Now That Reminds Me......

Carol Burkholder

authorHOUSE®

AuthorHouse™
1663 Liberty Drive, Suite 200
Bloomington, IN 47403
www.authorhouse.com
Phone: 1-800-839-8640

First published by AuthorHouse 10/22/2008

ISBN: 978-1-4389-0740-6 (sc)
ISBN: 978-1-4389-0739-0 (hc)

Printed in the United States of America
Bloomington, Indiana

This book is printed on acid-free paper.

Table of Contents

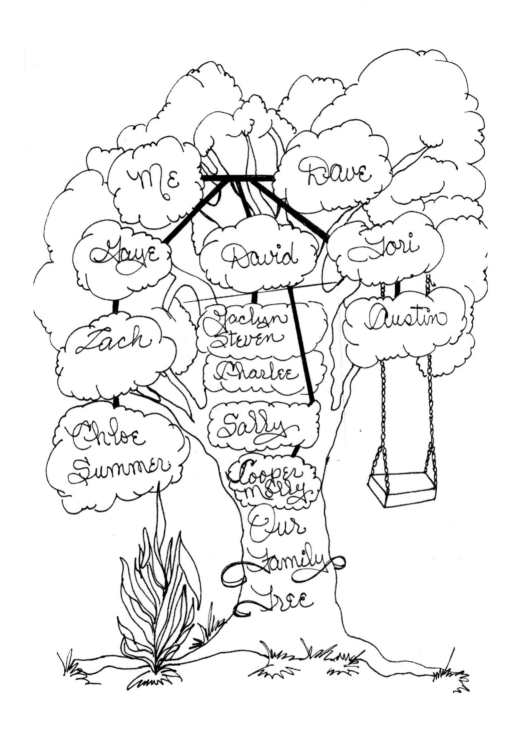

Our Family Tree

Preface: My style of writing leaves a lot to be desired, according to my college English teacher. When you start a project, she would say, do not use "the I" person. As I set down to put my thoughts to paper, that rule gets broken many times. It's an unconscious habit, an accident you might say. But this is how I, as the main character, tell the story. And when all is said and done, what remains is pretty much "MY" story. From my point of view, for sure. So, the style is me.

Sit back, fasten your seat belt, let's get to it!

Introduction: De-ja-vous---as far back as I can remember, when a seemingly common incident occurs; it will remind me of something that has happened before in my life. Even as a small child this was the case. Is it possible that I was born a reincarnate "Knock Off"? Or some such thing? Do I subconsciously remember too much? One thing I am completely sure of is that I absolutely do not have a photographic memory. Those plays in high school proved that beyond a shadow of a doubt. I could not remember even the smallest parts. Well, maybe I'd better rethink that statement; I was pretty good as Juliet in the death scene.

Maybe, perhaps, could it be that I have done and seen a great many repetitious things in my lifetime. Is it possible, or is every one a reactionary like me, however they are so busy the incident is just accepted? When I was growing up, we tried to dismiss that feeling. We called it someone stepping on our grave. To remove it, you would take three steps backward, jump up in the air once and start your walk over to erase the feeling. Those periodical repeat performances were forgotten and you would just move on.

Even now, I don't seam to be able to forget even the smallest if incidents. Maybe if I share some of them with you, we can laugh at them together, and then move on.

I have heard for years, from friends and family alike, "You should write a book." Whether or not they were serious or just trying to shut me up at the time is still a mystery.

We can check back on this topic later.

This book is dedicated to: Gaye, David, Tori

Edited by: J. Stancil

G.Horn and T. Sprunger

The Announcement

*Chapter one:..*Now that reminds me..

As I sit here at the computer and look at the blank page, yes, the blank page reminds me of an evening that started as any other evening had, during my fifty first year. Except that my husband of thirty-two years dropped dead of a massive heart attack. When I put it on paper, it looks as if I am being blaze. I truly am not, but it is much easier to write it than it was to live.

Dave was my first true love and we had been married for thirty two years. In any period of history, that is a feat in itself. But we really, no kidding, were in love. And still in lust in that thirty second year. Hard to believe, I know. Dave was adorable, all the girls in high school said so, black hair, jeans, white t-shirt, (he couldn't afford a leather jacket), so he wore a macho windbreaker, (but only when the temperature was below freezing). Otherwise he wore the t-shirt with the left sleeve rolled up so his smokes wouldn't fall out. He had a hair cut that was called the Detroit with a waterfall in the front. And the proverbial duck tails in the back that he adjusted each time he passed a mirror or a reflective piece of glass anywhere. It was too cool.

He was very intelligent, but he had dyslexia which caused him some learning problems. He had to work twice as hard as the other kids to, as they would say, get it. Not too many people knew what it was in the fifties. And even fewer knew how to deal with it. He didn't understand it either, so he acted like the rebel to cover up. Always the life of the shindig, he was the first one invited to all the parties. Totally the great dancer, all eyes were on him and his partner when he stepped up to dance. What a ladies man, he knew what to say to a girl to make her giddy. He was a year ahead of me in school and went to Central High, which was our rival school. I went to South High. The city fathers of Lima, Ohio decided to combine the two schools into one large high school.

The new school was named Lima Senior High School. What a huge travesty we all thought it was. We had been rivals in everything and without a second thought; they threw us all into a cauldron of boiling water. Well, the steam did rise that first year. Because of new class assignments, we started to form new friendships. And you guessed it; we were brought together as the seating arrangements changed.

I started dating one of Dave's close friends. We were a group of four guys and four girls before football season was over. One of my girl friends was dating Dave and we (the gang) hung out together as often as we could. I had a part time job on weekends and after school. The job was downtown about three blocks from the local YMCA. In the basement of that building was a teenage club, called the Yacht Club, where quite a few kids that I knew hung out. So on my way home from work, I'd stop in and have a soda and talk. We would all meet there whenever we could.

One evening, as Dave and I waited for the rest of the kids to arrive he decided to teach me how to fast dance. He thought I had potential. We had such a good time dancing together that it changed our choice of dating partners too. Soon we were an item, but the rest of the school was not as quick to accept the new high school as we had been.

There were still problems like: dress codes (We formed a subtle protest group. Every Friday, the girls would wear black, and the guys would wear their jeans inside out, rolled up to the knees. We never had to wear uniforms, and so we all felt like winners. But we were glad when we could wear other colors on Friday), school colors, integrating class subjects that had been taught at one school and not the other. Strange as it may seam, these problems united students and teachers. For the first time in our young lives, the teaching staff was in limbo with us.

Dave and his best friends decided they were getting out of there, and arranged to meet at the army recruiter to check out the options. Well, Dave and one other guy got there a little early. When they arrived, the army recruiter was not in his office. However, the Air Force recruiter was in, so they talked to him. He must have been quite a talker, because they signed up that very day. When the others came by, most of them had decided that the school was "not so bad" and went home. One of his friends signed up with the Marine recruiter. What a shock! And no one signed with the Army recruiter.

Now on this day, so many years later, another more sinister shock was unfolding. Just two weeks before Dave had undergone a battery of tests designed to assure us that the recent pains in his chest were not leading to a heart attack. Dave had been under the care of a flight doctor during his thirty two years in the Air Force. He had a heart murmur that had never caused him any physical discomfort or pain before. His father had died of a heart attack at a young age. The possibility of dying young was constantly on Dave's mind. More so, since he had retired. He still went to the base near by each year for a check-up and tests.

This particular evening started very innocently and turned into a total nightmare. I was standing over the stove, cooking Dave's favorite meal, pork chops and applesauce. I had browned the chops in the "iron skillet" that my grandmother had given me. An heirloom that had been in our family since she was a girl. The entire family agreed that food cooked in an old iron skillet was the greatest food of all. The next step was to add the sauerkraut, onions and a couple of apple slices. A main course I had picked up when we were stationed in Wiesbaden, Germany many years before. While the chops were simmering, I would peel and slice the potatoes, fry them in our "other iron skillet." The one that my mother had given me. This skillet was also in the family for many years, a little newer than the "number one iron skillet" though. (I will admit that at times the strangest things sometimes make me feel rich.) That evening it was the fact that we had two iron skillets. I didn't know anyone else in our circle of friends that was so blessed, by having two iron skillets. As I stood there in the middle of the kitchen feeling so very, very wealthy, the grandchildren came galloping in. That reminded me that it was time to stop daydreaming and put the biscuits in the oven, then warm the green beans. Of course there was applesauce for desert. Easy because the prep time was short. Just put some in the deserts cups and chill. All the while, my grandchildren Zach (he was five) and Austin (she was almost two, her birthday was in a couple of days) were continuing to playing tag up and down the hall, with an occasional run into the kitchen to circle around me and then they were off down the hall again, laughing and hollering. I just had to tell them that they needed to cheer up; they were acting and sounding too sad. They laughed and Zach said, "Gram is so funny".

About that time Dave came in from work, and started playing with the kids. He walked over to me, gave me a quick squeeze from behind, then checked the dinner and said how great it smelled. He said he was starving, and excused himself from the room for a minute.

As he started to leave, he hesitated, just for a second. I sensed him still behind me, and turned toward him. I thought he was going to notice my new blouse, or ask how the boy scouts meeting had gone, but he stopped, smiled, turned and left the room. I still pause from time to time and wonder what he was going to say. I so wish I knew. It is a haunting thing, even all these years later.

I took the biscuits out of the oven and checked the rest of the dinner, which was just about ready. Dave had not returned to the kitchen, so the little ones thought he was playing hide and seek. They took off yelling for him, the challenge was on. They couldn't find him, so they asked me to join in the search. I turned off the stove and nervously entered in the game. I knew that they were aware of all the best hiding places in the small house, but surely I could find him. He was not in the hall behind any door, not in the backyard in his favorite lawn chair, not in the bathroom, or any of the bedrooms.

Just then, my youngest daughter burst in thru the front door wanting to know if her dad was alright. I told her that we were just looking for him, but couldn't find him. I was sure he was somewhere close. She startled me because; she was scheduled to be at work. She asked me to take the kids out into the back yard while she conducted a search. Since she was a security guard at the local college, and had just been discharged from the Army, where she was a military police officer, I was pretty sure she could find him. She sounded so serious, I was starting to worry----a lot.

It was just a few seconds later when she came to the back door, told me to leave the children there in the backyard, go into my bedroom, and she headed for the phone. When I got to my bedroom, I still did not see Dave. I started over to the bed, and glanced at the closet, where I saw his feet. I really lost it, ran over to him and tried to feel a pulse. When I didn't find one, I started pounding on his chest, gathered myself, (hadn't I taken a class in CPR as a girl scout leader? Now was the time to put it into practice, not panic)

I took a deep breath and started CPR. My daughter (Tori, the youngest) came into the room and gently helped me to my feet. Through a fog, I heard her saying that an ambulance was on the way. She very quietly told me that what I was attempting was not going to work.

About this time my oldest daughter (Gaye) came in from work to a bizarre sight. Tori quickly told her what had just happened. As calmly as she could, she brought the kids in from the back yard, took them into another bedroom, and began to read them a story. Mainly to keep them out of sight of the ambulance and the techs that was taking their grandfather to the base hospital.

And that was the last time we ever saw him. I was so proud of both daughters, they were great, and handled the situation just right. I was, on the other hand, a basket case. They called my son (David) and told him what had happened. He was in the Air Force at the time. He and his wife came home in time for the funeral.

When I regained my senses, I asked Tori how she knew that there was something wrong. She told us that while she was at work, she got the most awful feeling that her father needed her. So she told her boss how she was feeling and he didn't even hesitate, he sent her home. She must have had a really intense look on her face as she stood before him. She was on the right track we did need her, but to this day, we have no idea how she knew. Her timing was almost perfect; she found her father, assessed the situation and headed for the phone. She called the base emergency room. When finally someone answered, he told her that the base ambulance didn't go off base for emergencies. What? She couldn't believe her ears, but had no time to argue. She hung up and called the local hospital, gave them the needed information, address etc. Then she turned her attention to me and the children. And Gaye's arrival was very welcomed also. They are both incredible to have around in a crisis situation. I feel very lucky that they were there to see me through. My son responded so quickly, he was there in two days. Support of your family is so important in this type of disaster, but it was most important to me after having over twenty years of "angst" every time Dave left the house.

My thought on this day was that our retirement plans were going to come true. He was out of the Air Force, he had just had a positive check up at the base, and things were on track for us to sit in those rocking chairs. The mere thought of him not being in that chair was unfathomable.

When I said before that we never saw Dave again, it was because he had specified in his will that he was to be cremated. So at the funeral we had the "Urn" and a collage of his pictures that spanned his life both civilian and military. The funeral was at the base chapel, and at the close of the service they played "taps and presented me with the flag".

My brother John only said one thing. He said that Dave and I were like bookends, he couldn't imagine one of us without the other.

The first time Dave and I were apart, when he went off to basic training, we pledged to look into the sky each evening at eight pm and say good night to each other. So, I bought him a star in the constellation Gemini (his astrological sign). Even now, I can continue the pledge that we set so long ago. It sounds corny, but we humans are a visual group and it helps me so much to have that star, with his name on it, which I can talk to.

I miss the way he would sip his morning coffee and read me the paper while I puttered around the kitchen. Then we would solve the problems of the world together before we went off to work. I miss the touching. Dave and I never passed each other without a touch. It is such a small gesture, but I miss it most of all.

Dating in the "50's"

Chapter two:..Now that reminds me..

Not too long ago, the president of our church choir got married to a nice young man who is also a member of our choir. They asked the remainder of the choir to sing at the wedding. It was so exciting, we all agreed rather quickly. As I sat there watching a friend walk down the aisle, looking beautiful and extremely happy, and my thoughts strayed for a moment back to my wedding day.

And that reminded me........ I remembered the same happy feeling and the look on my face said "I am totally happy and at the same time totally terrified."

Dave and I were married on Father's day June 17, 1956. The marriage lasted until April 24, 1988. We became sweethearts in high school. While I went into the senior year of high school, he joined the Air Force and went off to basic training in New York state.

After basic, he went on to Airborne Radio Communications School in Mississippi. He sent my name in Morse code every morning before class. It kept him focused, he said. But I think he did it because it was against the rules, and he was a rebel, you know.

At the end of a year in the service his training was complete and he had his first assignment to a base in S. Carolina.

While he was gone in Mississippi, I really missed him and I wrote my one and only "love letter". It was about ten pages long. I poured out my heart and recounted how we had met and why I picked him over anyone I'd met before. Why I wanted to wait until marriage before having sex, and the plans that I'd set up for the rest of my life. He kept the letter and apparently carried it with him for the remainder of his life. When my daughters were going through his belongings after his death, they found it. I didn't know he still had it, and still don't understand why he kept it. Was it to remind him of our beginnings? My romantic side wishes that he was planning to pull it out as we rocked on the front porch in our golden years and read it to me? I hope that was it!

Although I had missed all of his graduation ceremonies, he came to my high school graduation. When he arrived, he started telling everyone that he had come to collect me, and sweep me off to his uncle's camp in S. Carolina, (Uncle Sam, that is.) He had two weeks to complete his mission. In that two weeks of leave, I graduated from high school;

he was my escort at a Local Spring Time Parade and Ball (sponsored by the local YWCA and co-supported by some local businesses). A couple of those businesses were car dealers who let us ride in new convertibles during the parade. I was in the contest from my high school for princess of the parade. I didn't win, but I did come in third. We got to pick the convertible that we wanted to ride in with our escorts. Dave and I chose the beautiful blue Pontiac.

Sitting up on the back seat with the top down and my very own special Prince setting next to me gave the afternoon a truly magical feel. We were on our way to a new life together and, jump back jack, we were anticipating lots of adventures. It was the happy ending that we had seen in the movies. But the movie wasn't over for us. We were about to write another chapter with a new beginning. Who could ask for anything else? Of course we all had our picture taken for the local newspaper. I so totally felt like, for one night, I was the princess. The ballroom was decorated with crepe paper, which we had hung the day before. And of course we had the multifaceted ball hanging from the ceiling. This night was truly magical, and it was also "my prom night." Dave was in Mississippi training when the real prom night was in full swing, so I didn't attend. This night made it all OK.

The next day my husband to be, signed for me to get my drivers license, as I was still only sixteen. My mom sold us a car for a dollar. It was a blue and gray Pontiac, 1946, in perfect, or as we used to say, mint condition. We loaded it down with all of my art supplies, clothes, dishes, etc. Then, on Sunday we got married in my church, down the street from my mom's house; had the reception in her back yard; danced the night away; met all of each others relatives; picked out names for our children; discussed the condition of the world (even had the answer to world peace). The next day, bright and early we "took-off for the South".

Now I had been as far east as New York City, as far north as the Goolie River in Canada, but the furthest south I had been was Kentucky. Was I in for a huge SURPRISE, or what? However my traveling companion and husband had been as far south as Mississippi. He was also a whole year older than me. He was my hero in that cool uniform, my knight in shinning armor. We jokingly told our friends, as we left, we were spending our honeymoon at Dave's uncle's camp in S. Carolina. It really sounded funny when we said it.

By late the next day we had arrived at the only motel in the small southern town near the base. After checking in and calling the base to let his commander know he had returned with me and my belongings in tow, we laid there in the dark watching the flashing neon sign in front of the motel. Remember, this was 1956. The grocery stores were closed for the evening. The highway through three mountain ranges had been two lanes. There were three roadside parks with outhouse type restrooms in the whole six hundred miles. No fast food places that you saw from the highway. And it was so very far between gas stations. Dave and I took turns driving and sleeping. It was quite an adventure for my first outing as a new bride. Somewhere during that first few hours of married life, I felt so grown up, so worldly. If I could make this trip and still smile, I could do anything.

The first thing I wanted that evening was a bubble bath. I was new at this marriage deal. Dave needed to use the bathroom, and I was in the tub (a tub without a curtain at all), I made him wait until I was finished with my bath and in my robe before he could come into the bathroom. He got a little out of sorts, and yelled, "We are married you know". I found it hard to adjust so quickly from, no touchy feely to, let's get naked and play house.

Well, it is true that he had three brothers and a younger sister to share a bathroom with. While I was the oldest in my family with two younger brothers. So, I was used to getting my solitary bath time first and not sharing with anyone. I was tired and cranky, and didn't want to share this quiet time with anyone (not even Dave). It is not a good idea to be selfish right off the bat, if you want a successful marriage. I felt really bad about my actions when I saw his sad, puppy dog look as I came out of the bathroom. Wow, did I have a lot to learn. In the story of the happy princess, everything was perfect after the couple drives off into the sunset.

I never really thought that part out (I guess I thought it would take care of itself, not need an assist from me). Oh yes, I sure was wise and worldly. Wait, the way to a man's heart and forgiveness is through his stomach. I had it all figured out. My mom had packed us some food for the trip. I knew exactly where it was, my problem was solved. Except that when I got to the car, I discovered that we had already devoured it, eaten everything. We were destined to go to bed hungry.

What a wedding trip. We just laid there in the light of the neon sign for the longest time holding on to each other. How could we fold at the first sign of hunger. Didn't we still have each other? The laughter was a little nervous, but it broke the tension and the whole situation didn't seem so hopeless. I'm sure that although Dave was trying to comfort me, he was thinking back to the wedding.

His brother Tom had offered to cover for him if he wanted to run and not go through with the wedding. Dave had started sweating like the proverbial pig, and Tom was sure that meant that he was terrified. But Dave explained to him that the whole thing was his idea. He not only wanted to get married, he wanted to be married to me. He had given me his mom's wedding ring to wear forever. Which, by the way, was not to popular with the rest of his family. I looked too young and frivolous to them. But Dave was sure that this was the right way to spend the rest of his life. The Air Force, I and whatever came after. He assured everyone on his side of the aisle that this marriage would last, as the preacher says, "till death do us part." Yep, he was my hero! That night at the motel, we laughed at the whole world, and made a pact to set out on our own personal adventure. We would discover the world and share our conclusions with each other. We'd also set out to discover everything about each other. We planned how we would grow old together, sitting in dual rocking chairs on the porch and recounting our adventures. We would grow old gracefully, and in the country where all of our children, grandchildren, and oh yea, even our great grandchildren could gather on holidays just to tell us of their adventures and successes. We looked at each other and mutually agreed that we should immediately start the discovery of each other .That was a quite good decision.

But his untimely death that evening in April gave me an unbelievable emptiness. The anger welled up in me. He had bailed on me. All of our plans were cancelled there on the floor.

I have sat on the porch lately, as the plan went. We had both decided how it would be early in our marriage. I've rocked in my chair and told our story to the brick wall. I am here to testify that it is not the same as having Dave sitting in the other rocker. However I have tenderly placed his ashes, which occupy the stately marble urn, in the rocker next to me. I so want to shout skyward at the top of , my lungs--- So there!!!!

Chapter three: Now that reminds me………

I have always thought of myself as an ordinary housewife, with an extraordinary life. I feel very fortunate to have spent sixty nine years on this extraordinary planet. I have been up, down, loved, trod upon, cheered, jeered, revered, misunderstood, pushed, pulled, poked, prodded, handled with velvet gloves, attacked by a truck (which by the way, the truck won that battle). I have been rich and I have been poor. Trust me on this one, rich is better.

Over the years, we have collected furniture from many countries. Often there was a small amount of money and the piece of furniture was needed, so we would be sure that we didn't compromise. By that I mean, it must be the one of all the choices we found that we could live with forever. We would get a piece here and a piece there. The only prerequisite was that it must be a piece that we really liked. It has been amazing to me that although the pieces have no common origin, they go together like they were all purchased at the same time. I think that if you gather the furniture that is special to you, it will all come together. I lovingly call our furniture "early GI".

From time to time, I have attempted to rise above the ordinary and set out in search of the perfect me. I have been, for the most part, very outwardly happy and have been encouraging to others, friends as well as family. Looking on the brighter side of all and any situation. So much so that at times I have infuriated both friends and family alike with my "sunshine outlook". As I was reminiscing the other day, being myself , it reminded me of my life—because contrary to popular belief—your life does not wait until just before you die to flash before your eyes. As the years roll by, you sit and contemplate the previous events and times, and there it goes flashing before you in a series of short stories. Well it came to me during one such journey through the tulips, that my public image was not altogether as joyful as my name. Carol means, loosely translated, joyful song of God. Flashing before me were scenes of: me biting my nails(as we were traveling from place to place), grinding my teeth(as I was sleeping), and a twitch in my left eye(that I had developed in 1962 and lasted all the way through1999). It was granted an on and off thing, but was there none the less. WOW, what a Revelation! I have laughed at and yes, even taunted from time to time others with such afflictions. Now, I ask you, is that the behavior of a sweet happy-go-lucky God loving adult lady? I think not.

And that reminded me….. Dave had such a twitch. When he got nervous, his nose would twitch like a bunny. I thought it was cute, but I sure did tease him about it. And there was my uncle "Sport" (a great guy, and I loved him dearly). Well, when he got excited about something like catching a huge fish, or telling a story about my dad as they were growing up, he would start to spit. It was a kind of "raspberries" sound. I was always the first to burst into laughter, when he got started. In hindsight, I realize that was a form of viciousness that I had not realized was there inside of me. While I can not take it all back, I can change and modify (and apologize) my behavior for the future. Which I shall endeavor to do, starting now.

With all of the war news these days, death has become a normal topic. In the old days, We avoided talking about death, because we didn't want to think about the inevitable. But when the news starts in the evening, what I see on the screen reminds me that I have been close to death, more than once. Through all of these phases of my life, I never came close to realizing how incredibly horrible death leaves those who are still living. The reality of it all hit me like a ton of bricks on the day Dave died suddenly.

It really knocks your socks off!!!

To repeat it, I have been very fortunate in my life and times. Remember, I didn't say it has been boring (a favorite saying of my great granddaughters, Summer and Chloe). It is most difficult to know where to start my writing project. I am anxious to tell you what has been important to me so you can compare and contrast our lives. To me, that is a good deal of the fun of reading a book. Feeling a connection with the people on the pages. Come on, let us go on an adventure together.

And that reminds me ....of how important my children are to me. They have been the greatest adventure of my life, and have brought me the most joy. A close second to them would be my grandchildren, and not too long ago I was blessed with four adorable great grandchildren. When you contemplate (as is customary later on in life), you can plainly see what a great group we started in 1956. You can't see me, however, I am taking a bow.

Here I am as a youngster

Chapter four:..Now that reminds me of my beginning..

I was born to my loving parents in the dead of winter. A happy bald baby, who liked to sleep. So much so, that they had to wake me at meal time. My mother may not have had a million (I love to tell what Carol did stories) but she can come pretty close to that number on a good day. She loves to tell how, as a baby, I was what they call now-a-days, high maintenance. It seemed that I wanted to be the one that decided when everyone went to bed and when the household woke up each morning, Of course, the hours I picked were not the ones that the rest of the house wanted. I started out stubborn and hot tempered. Well, I was the first child, I guess that gave me the task of showing our parents who runs the house. I only hope my brothers appreciate what I did for them before they were born. Just kidding. I am told that as I grew, I became a pretty, sweet, intelligent toddler, oozing with affection. "There was no understanding of cares or worries in the rambunctious darling", my mother says. Those of her friends who were the parents of little toddler boys, would often complain to her about me chasing, hugging and kissing their little boys. Out of all of this toddler love, it was the constant germ spreading they disliked the most. So my mother, being the wise one that she is, got me a puppy.

My mother loves to tell another toddler story. It seams that I was an early bloomer, as they say, walking at seven months, never took a pacifier, was diaper trained at eight months and talking before the age of two. All of these qualities made me curious a lot earlier than I normally would or should have been. I was into everything and bothering the all adults around me with questions until they wanted to run when they saw me come. So, one day we went to visit my favorite aunt. As my mother and I walked in the front door, I yelled, "put away the crystal and run for the hills, here comes Carol". Of course, my mother was mortified (but everyone laughed), and it got the point across. And things got a little bit easier when we came in the door to visit. One of my mother's friends was a school teacher. She told my mother that I should go to her kindergarten class when I was three. So it was agreed that I would go and check it out. I stayed for the year.

By the time I was four, I was finishing the stories for the teacher. Yep, you're right, they sent me on to first grade. I have always loved school, thinking that is where all the action is. There is so much to learn, question and discuss, what better place to grow?

And that reminds me of another one…..

We lived in a small town in the middle of Ohio where it was so safe we didn't lock our doors. I had relatives all over the place, and was full of wanderlust, even at a young age. Well, one day, my mother said I was four, she was busy with my younger brother, so I walked downtown. I went into the feed store and saw a little red wagon. I said "hi" to everyone and took the red wagon home. It amuses me that they just said "bye" and watched me go. When I got home my mom was very annoyed with me, gathered up my brother, and marched me back to the store. She asked the owner of the store, why he had let me take it and he said, "why won't you let her have it"? Now, she was mad at both of us. But she wouldn't let me keep it, so we walked back home very slowly. A little girl that was a little sadder, but a little wiser.

My mother called me a few years ago to tell me that one of her older sisters had researched the family tree and discovered that some of our ancestors were on the Mayflower when it landed in the US all those many years ago. This was amazing news to me because when I was in high school, discoveries like this one were worthy to be printed in the local paper. They made a great deal of difference in social standing in the community. As my opportunity to utilize the information had passed, Dave and I told our friends that my ancestors had landed in the new land, and his ancestors were there to meet them. Our children and their children etc. were true Americans.

This tidbit of information stirred my oldest daughter and me to investigate further our ancestors on my father's side of the family. We found that the Scottish side of the family belongs to two clans, which authorizes us to wear two separate tartans. The Maxwell tartan which is red and green and the Douglas tartan which is blue and yellow. We have started attending the yearly gathering at nearby Grandfather Mt. We are learning as much as we can about our heritage. It is more and more interesting the more we discover. The yearly gathering of the clans lasts three days. The first day, each clan enters the valley and sets out their colors. In the evening they light signal fires on the mountain side. What a sight and the sound of the bagpipes playing in the still of the night. The next two days are filled with the dance and sporting competitions. Also the bagpipe band, playing and marching contests keep everyone entertained. In a hollow on the side of the mountain, there are the rock and folk bands playing. There are booths with Scottish food, clothing and other wares. By the third evening, everyone is pleasantly exhausted as the clans withdraw the colors and we all set off talking about who will win the contests next year.

We have also gone to the annual meeting at Stone Mountain in Georgia. The meeting at Estes Park, Colorado was the first one that we attended.

That was the one that started us investigating our heritage. When we were stationed in Europe we never had the opportunity to visit Scotland. A few years ago we took a trip to gather some background and soak up all the history and culture (sights, sounds, tastes and smells) that we could.

In Scotland, we spent some time at one of the old ancestral castles. It is totally self sustaining with its own stable, blacksmith, jeweler, seamstress, outdoor obstacle course, chapel, brewery, real growing maze, secret garden (where they serve afternoon tea, have beautiful statues, peacocks, and fragrant flowers). The entire estate is steeped in history at every turn. It was the place of refuge for Mary, Queen of Scots, when she was hiding from Elizabeth. It has the huge iron gates and entry way lined with awesome trees where the carriages of old entered the grounds. There are still a few of the guard huts that lined the estate in olden times. Huge yew trees line the river (where swans float in the afternoon) that runs behind the castle. And there are endless fields of Rhododendrons.

While we were there, a local theatrical company came and preformed a Shakespearean play around the castle. The audience followed the actors from scene to scene. Each scene was in a different location on the grounds. It was, to say the least, fastenating. I'm only sorry that we did not start looking into our past history sooner. The more we find about the past, the more we can understand about the present.

Chapter five:..Now that reminds me..

At the end of each year, there are always TV shows that feel compelled to show us what has happened in the year we have just left. They want to cover everything from A to Z. So we cannot forget, not only the new TV commercials of the year, but the international ones and the best commercials of all time. When my grandson Zach was very small, he helped me to remember which of these commercials my favorites were. He loved to go to the base commissary with me. As we shopped, we would start at one end and cover the store from wall to wall. Do you remember the commercial where there was a clean-up on each aisle as the people shopped? Well, thank goodness, we never had that particular problem. Instead we had a little boy standing in the aisle and serenading the patrons with the appropriate jingle of each product that he recognized on the shelves. He could belt it out from the front seat of the cart, just as easily. He was so talented. He loved commercials, not the shows in between, the commercials.

We got different reactions from the other shoppers. There were the mouths open as they passed us; the little snickers; the outright laughers; and the ones who were looking around for the cameras. It was fun for me, and it certainly made my shopping not only easier, but so much more exciting. Sometimes, I'd join in. It was really a good thing that we always had a grocery list, or I would have forgotten why I was there by the second aisle.

Now, it was back in the days of families eating dinner together. We shopped once or twice a month and shopped from a list with the meals planned. At dinner, we discussed everyone's day and planned the weekend schedules, so we wouldn't have too many conflicts. Whoa, that was so long ago. Now everyone eats when they are hungry, not because it is time to eat. There has been such a dramatic change in lifestyle and health concerns around this house. Some things haven't changed though, I still push the vitamins for everyone, everyday.

Some days while I am shopping, I catch myself humming a few jingles. I even find myself adding my own lyrics, to suit the mood of the day. On an exceptionally drab day, I could be caught doing the "teaberry shuffle" in the aisles of the grocery store. It's relatively simple, but puts a spark in your step. You are innocently walking along, and then you pause; jump up and when you land your feet are spread apart, then you jump again and kick your right leg behind you, repeat with your left leg, and then step forward on your right foot, back on your left foot and casually resume your walk. It is very invigorating.

Another fun way to perk you up as you shop is to take song titles and make sentences out of them. Example: Blue Moon and Smoke On the Water, Remind Me Of You. Try it, you'll find it a lot of fun.

Zach soon out grew his commercial jingle phase and switched to guitar lessons instead. He and a few of his friends started a band. I thought they were very good, but he gave it up for a woodworking class. Being in the always changing, and growing influential sphere of children helps to keep us young. I'm living proof. And, by the way, we still use the beautiful two-toned cutting board that Zach made for the kitchen in his wood shop class.

*Chapter six:..*Now that reminds me..

I was sitting here, typing on the computer when the phone rang. It was a friend from work who wanted to rehash the day. Let me ask you if you have ever been talking on the phone, and although you thought you were listening; maybe you even thought you were interested in what the other person was saying, you found yourself picking up a pencil and drawing lines (or little pictures) on a pad of paper? Well, that my friend is "doodling". It's a personal thing. But, it's also a people thing. People all over the world find themselves "doodling". We can use them to relieve tension or stress. Not so surprising. When we observe our doodles we can learn a lot about ourselves and our feelings. Many people dismiss them as a mindless act, but it's not mindless, it's subconscious.

What if we could find a constructive way to use them? Did you know there are a lot of popular types of doodles? For a long time, I thought my doodles were exclusively mine. Not so. Some of the more popular doodles are the basic shapes; circle, squares, flowers, arrows and stars.

Try to keep your doodles for a week, and see if you are a repeat doodler. See if you are an innovative doodler. Or see if you are an imaginative doodler.

Here are some tips for analyzing your week's worth of doodles. Check the shapes, sizes and directions that you have. Example: You have a doodle that looks like a huge scribble, you could have been angry at the person on the other end of the phone. Or maybe it was an unusually stressful day for you. As a painter, I like to loosen up with doodles, to see how I'm feeling. If I do tight circles, or lots of straight lines, I can constructively use that information to alter my strokes and change to large open circular motions. So when you find yourself doodling, check them out and use them to your advantage. Let them work for you, so to speak.

Let me leave you with this thought. You may find from your doodles that you are in the wrong career field. Some days I'd like to use my doodles as a painting, and then, of course, there are the other days.

Picture of doodles:

The first passport picture

*Chapter seven:..*Now that reminds me..

As the evening news begins, the first order of business is the war. As you can imagine that reminds me of my temporary duty as an Air Force wife. Temporary duty that extended into thirty two years. We were not at one base for the entire time. We were transferred regularly. Each time we got a new assignment, Dave and I realized it was a chance to have another adventure. Besides, if we were unhappy with the new base, it would only be temporary. We had each other, we had the kids, and we could do it standing on our heads. If you say "temporary duty" slow somehow there is something strangely comforting in those two words.

When life flows from ups to downs, or jolts you from highs to lows, you can cling to those words, swing from them, and then gently tuck them neatly under your pillow at sundown. They can save you in times of stress and give you that extra push or Oomph to forge to the front of the pack during a moment of indecision. Those words are all encompassing. When you are cleaning house (seems like a mundane and mostly mindless task) you can set those words to your favorite tune and "chant" the rooms of puppy fur, dust mites, spilled milk left on the night stand, and the yellow stain from the toilet seat away. As an accomplished veteran of this practice, I can uncatagoricly state that it works on all types of music from Beethoven's Fifth to Rap. Give it a try and you will see for yourself how amazing it is. When you become accomplished at this chanting, you will find yourself starting to dance around the rooms and, dare I say it, having fun.

I didn't even dare to tell my best friends, they already thought I was a little weird. But then, we wouldn't be there long enough to start a good rumor, even if my secret was discovered. Many days have come and gone since I indulged in those words, but the feeling still lingers. Temporary duty is truly an amazing phrase.

And telling you that story, well.........that reminds me......

of one event we had during the early sixties, Dave was assigned to an Air Force base just outside of Wiesbaden, Germany and of course I wasn't going to be left behind. I had signed on to go wherever he went (as far as I could you understand). We were stationed in South Carolina at the time, and so we packed up our belongings, stashed them in my grandma's attic in Ohio, visited with mom and family, and got our passports. Dave went on ahead to find us a place to live. In

South Carolina we had given birth to three beautiful babies and they caught the excitement bug about moving. It took him three months to find us a place. There was no space for us in the base housing complex, and the wait for us to move in was a year and a half. I didn't want to wait that long, so he found us an apartment in a three story house in small village off the base. We would have the bottom floor, two nuns the second, and the family that owned the house would have the top floor. We were the only Americans in the village, so it was an adventure for all of us in the village.

What an adventure it was to get to Germany. We were excited and ready. So, we hopped on a plane and went to meet Dave and Europe. We flew in a "SMALL", puddle hopper plane from Ohio to New Jersey. The trip was fairly smooth and short. The next day we caught a really "LARGE" plane to Newfoundland (where everything was covered in snow). It was very beautiful but we didn't get to stay there too long, just about long enough to throw a snowball. It was a break before the longest part of the journey. Then it was on to Europe.

We saw England (London), the first capital city, and then over Paris and onto Wiesbaden. The children thought it was the most fun ever. They especially liked watching the boats that were so small in the ocean they looked like toys in a bathtub. Meanwhile I was borrowing all the burp bags I and my helper could find. What a way to find out I get air

46

sick. When we boarded the plane in New Jersey, the pilot assigned a lieutenant to assist me, since I had three small ones. I was truly grateful before long that he was there. What an unforgettable huge help it was to us, especially me. I never even got a chance to thank him, for he disappeared as soon as we were out of the plane and in the terminal. It is possible that he was so exhausted, he faded away. Just kidding! But it is still a big regret that I never got the chance to thank him.

SO, GEORGE, WHERE EVER YOU ARE, WE THANK YOU VERY MUCH !!!!!!!!

This is really how they took off the gloves after a flight. Dave is on the left.

Chapter eight..Now that reminds me..

As the war in Iraq goes on, we are seeing more and more stories of the families of the fighting men. The hardest part of being left behind by these gallant guys and gals is the daily worry of those who wait for their return. On TV we see the brave departures and the triumphant returns, but the day to day waiting, the worry and tension, is the reality of those waiting. These stories remind me of the families that were in Europe, in the sixties and seventies, less the support that they would have had by waiting for their loved ones in the US. Some of the families were torn apart by the service member being sent to the front lines while they waited in a foreign country. The other families there were very supportive and helpful, but it was still easy to feel alone.

Some wives and children returned to the US and waited there. Some commanders required the families to return to the US, knowing, from experience that the strain was too intense on the families. But there were those who hung in there, waited and huddled together because of the need to be close enough to get all the news, to be close enough to talk to their spouses from time to time. When the planes were flying they would patch phone calls back to the base, to talk to the wives and kids. Also when the troops would rotate in and out of war torn areas, you could receive news of your loved ones, first hand.

We were stationed in Germany, during those days. We had three small children and I had been a part of the Air Force community for ten years by then. By this time in our lives, even though I was in my late twenties, I was considered an old hand. As a dutiful wife, I was at Dave's side, as close as I could be that is. He was on flying status, and gone more than he was at home. He flew to exotic places on important missions, but with three small children and a job on base, I was pretty busy too.

In the states it was a time of free love, peace marches, and young girls passing out flowers to young men with large hormone problems. There were many young men leaving home for the first time and coming to the land of brotchen, free flowing wine and loose women. Some of the loose women were military wives who were also away from their home for the first time. Excited about seeing far off places, but also frightened when their young men brought them to Europe and then boarded the huge 130's and left for Greece, Spain and Africa's sunny shores. They were faced with the task of keeping busy until the planes that look like overgrown bees returned.

The young airmen returned with such stories that many wives became jealous of their mates. Some set out to have flings of their own with the airmen that waited their turn to board the planes and fly off. Some sat in their apartment and never left for weeks at a time. These young ladies did not last long and went back home to mother across the big pond. I and some of the other old hands, tried to encourage the younger wives to keep busy, take tours, and take up a couple of local pastimes, like hiking and knitting. We had a wives club and we raised money for the younger couples with small children who were having financial difficulties. Germany while a very beautiful country, is also a very expensive country. Our plans worked to a certain degree, but there were still some problems.

So this is where the "Butterfly Project" came into all of our lives. I was doing a lot of sewing, as two of our children were girls. I made a lot of their clothes and mine too. Before I left the states, and headed for Europe, my mom and I stocked up on a bunch of sewing knick-knacks. We had no idea of what to expect in the stores and shops of what we knew as ancient cultures.

We tried to buy small, modern notions that I could carry in our suitcases. Things like buttons, elastic, ornaments, cloth frogs, butterflies, flowers and so on. Well, one evening I had this brilliant idea, at least I thought it was. I could have a special heart to heart chat with each new girl as a part of their welcome to the base. At a lunch for the new arrival, I would take her aside and tell her confidentially how I was excited, frightened and very apprehensive about my first trip away from the US, my home and family. I would tell her that our first assignment was a small island about five hundred miles off the coast of Portugal. It measured seventeen miles wide and twenty seven miles long. It was a truly beautiful place.

When we stood on the top of the mountains we could see water on all sides of the island.

What an awesome feeling! We explored the water caves; the beaches with their black sand; the old fort as it lay in ruins; and the hiking trails left by the farmers who brought their crops to market. We shopped in the local stores and tried to learn Portuguese. We found it, for the most part, to be a very difficult language.

While shopping in the village one day, I came across a golden butterfly pin. The shop was small and not too well lit. In the corner of the shop, sat a little old lady in a red and black shawl. In her broken English she proceeded to tell me a story of how I was like that butterfly. In as much as I could understand she said that as the caterpillar, I too had grown near my parents and home. As I left the warmth of my home to come to this far away island, I felt alone and isolated, as when the

52

caterpillar cocoons. But now was the time for me to learn and grow in a new country, stretching my wings as I emerge from that cocoon and become the beautiful butterfly I was meant to be. What a wise lady she was. We laughed a little and wept a little together. She gave me the butterfly pin, and wished good things for me. I sat there quietly for a moment. And then I smiled, yes, I was emerging from that cocoon. I put the pin on my jacket lapel.

At this point in my chat with the young wife, I would take the golden butterfly pin off my jacket and place it in her hand. I would tell her I wanted her to be reminded that she too was like that butterfly. She must grow with this opportunity, not be afraid of it. We would share a smile and a tear, and bond a little.

Now, I'm not going to say that I saved all the young wives, but I did hope I helped a little to get some of them off on the right foot. Then, when the next young lady arrived, I'd go to my sewing basket and take out another golden butterfly, put it on my jacket lapel and go to greet her. That was, as you know many years ago. I had forgotten about it.

Last week, as I was going through my jewelry with one of my granddaughters, looking for something special for her to wear. I found the last golden butterfly. I still have one. I will always keep this one nearby. From time to time that little golden butterfly has been a reminder of how I have learned and grown by helping others.

In our own ways, and as an extension of our loved ones, we (the wives) became fighting guys too. The butterfly pin helped us to envision our goal toward success.

Chapter nine:..Now that reminds me..

A new type of diet is in the news today. I am always one of the first ones in line to try a new diet. It has been so since I was a teenager. Sometimes, a new one comes on the scene before I have had a chance to reject the previous one. I have always worked on my image, to make myself a better person. I have tried horoscopes, yoga, transindental meditation, ZEN, numerology, the gym, tai chi, the total gym, enlightenment classes, and every diet known to man. Yep, I have tried it all. If all those things had worked, or even some of them had worked, I'd be president now. For a person that has not felt very experimental (just your average in all things kind of person) I have used most of my years, and energy trying to become the totally perfect person, wife and mother. But I have failed because in my search for perfection. I cracked, somewhere in the mix, I slipped to include lying and even infidelity.

Now that reminds me........

Lies, where is the line? As a good Christian woman, I have always told others not to lie. But the truth is that, until recently, I truly believed in using little white lies when the occasion called for them. Dave's family has said that I was too good for him. And there was a time that I feared I would go to heaven when I died, and Dave would most certainly go to hell. How can we spend eternity together if that were the case? My view of eternity has been altered in the last few years. Now, I see us in a large room separated by a sheet of glass. We can see each other, but not touch. That is hell in it's rarest form.

Of course, the first reaction is that there is a way over, under, around or through that glass. In our wills, we both have requested to be cremated. So we can be together. Does this change, or rearrange the life after death situation? By that, I mean, will we both go to heaven, or hell? I'll try to let you know later.

An interesting fact about cremation is that the Vikings burned their dead as a tribute to their loved ones. Across the world, where the oriental people did not know of the existence of the Vikings, they had the same ritual. I, too, am in favor of cremation. For a while after Dave was cremated, I took his urn with me when I traveled. I have mellowed somewhat in the last few years. I have decided that he has logged enough miles in his life and since his death, that he deserves a rest. I have teased the children that they must have our ashes mingled and put into three urns. So our ashes can be together, and a part of us can be with all of them. It will be interesting to see what happens to us in the future.

Here is an incident from the past. One summer, Zach and I left Dave's urn at David Lee's house in Little Rock. We had just spent a couple of weeks with David and his family and were traveling on to Tennessee. There we would visit with Zach's other grandparents and to join up with Gaye. Then we would go on to Ohio and visit my mom.

We would complete the circle by coming back to North Carolina. By then the summer would be at an end and we would have many things to talk over for months to come. We had placed the urn in the center of the back seat for the whole trip. But, it was late and we were anxious to get on the road. Both of us forgot to double check the back seat. About twenty miles down the road, I looked up at the rear view mirror, and there was the empty back seat. So, we turned around and trekked back to David's house. I knocked (quietly because it was eleven PM) and the door opened instantaneously. There stood David with the urn in his hands. We all burst into laughter (David said, "Love you"), we got in the car, gently placed Dave in the middle of the back seat, and quietly sped away. It was a very interesting summer for us, and we were glad to be back in NC. So happy that we remembered Dave on each of the remaining stops, that special summer trip.

Chapter ten:...... Now that reminds me.....

It is difficult to predict what will trigger a memory. There are obvious times, like when you see a couple walking hand in hand. You'll remember you and your soul mate doing the same. Maybe it will remind you of the boy whose hand you rejected in grade school because he teased your friend and had no remorse. Perhaps one of your children asks a basic, innocent question. A friend, at lunch rehashes the morning's activities. Or even a great grandchild, redirects your attention to nature. When Chloe (my oldest great grandchild) finds the butterfly that landed on the clover in the front yard, and quietly lies down beside it to get a better look. Or when Summer (her twin sister) can find the plane that you have to squint to see among the clouds, and will make the buzzing sound that no one but she can hear. It's the feeling that comes over you and transports you to another time in your life, perhaps happy: perhaps sad:, perhaps a little of both, but in a split second, and uncontrollably, you are there. Some days a plethora of memories run thru your mind. It is as if your whole body is in fast forward, or reverse motion. It catches your brain off guard.

The jolt, to the outside world, looks as if you have spaced out. Any explanation on your part is met with a smile, and quite often a "sure" or "right". And all you can think of is, "boy, they would never believe this". What a dog gone shame if that saying is true, "the mind is the first thing to go". Not so much of a shame if it takes you with it, of course.

How about when you go out to check the mail. Someone has been on vacation and has sent you a postcard. Now I love postcards because you get the bonus of a beautiful scene on the front, or a cartoon to show that the vacation is going well. And to let you know you are not having as good a time as they are, just to perk up your dreary day. They are inexpensive, you can send a short but sweet message, and they are easy to fill. You can write up the side to show that you want to write more if only you had the space.

But did you know that they are potentially dangerous? Well, when Dave went off to basic training, I got hooked on postcards. I'd say

"Hi" ask how he was, and fill the rest of the card with a cute joke, send my love, and poof, I was done. I did not know that the drill instructor handed out the mail. He got a real kick out of reading the postcards to all the troops as he handed them out. He particularly loved my postcards. How incredibly mortifying it must have been for Dave. Especially when the jokes were lame. I was not especially good at jokes, but I thought I was. Sometimes the jokes were a little bit off and I was so naïve that I didn't catch the double entandre.

Example: In Eskimo, too pooped to pop means to numb to come. Enough said??? We had been married about ten years before Dave could tell me what had happened with my postcard pheasco. Only then could we laugh about it. I still enjoy sending and receiving postcards. However, I am very careful what is written on them. Please remember to keep a "positive attitude" and "sense of humor" handy.

Then I am reminded of the time that postcards were very helpful to us. On one of our cross country trips, from Florida to California, we passed the Painted Desert. Dave didn't want to wait until daylight so we could enjoy the spender of those painted hills, so we drove on past them in total darkness. The next morning, at the first gas station we could find, I bought postcards for our photo album.

Chapter eleven:..<u>Now That Reminds Me..</u>

I was flipping thru the channels the other day, and caught a soap opera that was focused on a couple that turned out to be married to different people in the show. They were in "grand flagante delecto". And you know what affect that had on me.

Now that reminds me...........

When you are far away from home, say across the Atlantic Ocean. Or maybe on an Island in the Atlantic Ocean. It is easy to fall from grace. I gave my life to God at the tender age of eight. No, this is not a sermon. But, there was a time when I did turn away from my religion and almost lost all that I held and still hold dear. I became, what I'd call irrational and simultaneously, a hypocrite. Let me give you a little background:

During my teenage years, I was steadfast and strong in my approach to maturity. All things were strictly black and white, no gray in sight. I was president of my church youth group. I was a Red Cross volunteer. I was the secretary of the local chapter of the Youth Temperance Organization. I was an "A" student. On my free period at school, I worked in the school office. I never kissed on the first date, and slammed anyone who did that sort of thing. When I left home to follow Dave in his dream of a career in the Air Force, I was loyal to him completely. I joined the local military church, and helped the wives club with troubled wives away from home for the first time. We had young airmen over for holidays, so they wouldn't feel so alone. I was not taken in by the little flirtations that seem to follow young men when they leave home and become part of the elite force (Air Force). I was flattered by the attention. I was a mother of three before I turned twenty, and frankly, didn't feel very glamorous. But that was as far as it ever went. So then, what leads a person to veer so incredibly far to the left? I am still pondering and a little sick in the stomach when it floods back to me.

At the time we were on an island five hundred miles off the coast of Portugal. The Island was way too small for the two thousand Americans that were stationed there. There was Air Force and Navy personnel, of course, a small detachment of each Army and Marine personnel, Portuguese and American civilian workers, and a detachment each of Portuguese and American military police to ease tensions between the villagers and the US dependents. Now, I was not a novice at the military wife lifestyle by this time in my life.

Dave and I had been married for over eleven years and had been at bases stateside, in South Carolina, Florida and California, as well as bases in Europe at Frankfurt, Wiesbaden, and Spangdahlem Germany.

So what was so different here? The tour of duty started off rather smoothly. We found a house on a hill, off base. The kids went to school on base.

Dave and I both joined the local Red Cross (he as a swimming instructor, and I as a hospital volunteer). We joined the bowling leagues, the base gym (complete with steam room and an on duty masseuse). Things were going well, I was even asked to do an early morning talk show on Armed Forces Radio. I nervously accepted, and found it so exciting. I had a great time doing the show, It was basically aimed at the US female population on the islands. Everyday, the ticker tape came in from the Armed Forces Radio Organization in the US, giving me the latest femine news and trends back home.

Soon I had people stopping me and asking if I could get information from the US for them. They would also ask if I knew what was going back home on a particular subject. (examples: how was the flower power movement affecting the military? What was the latest popular shade of lipstick, etc.) It was really a lot of fun (and more work than I anticipated). As time went on, I was working (it was all volunteer work) more and more.

One day, Dave walked into the NCO Club and put a notice on the bulletin board that said, " If anyone sees my wife, please have her call me, so I can make an appointment to see her". This was a wake up call for me. So, I slowed down on the radio bit, and stuck to scouting (girl and boy), hospital volunteering and wives club. We found a replacement on the radio show, and started a wives volley ball league. Dave was one of the coaches, so we spent a lot of time together for the remainder of the tour.

Oh, I almost forgot, to tell you about my problem. It would seam that I was so busy, that I couldn't squeeze in an affair. But not me. I really did it. It just sort of snuck up on me. I told you that Dave and I had joined a bowling league. Well, we joined three leagues. We lived on an island in the Atlantic, and there were days when the winds, or the winds and the storms were so strong that planes couldn't take off or land. We had to have something to do during those times so, we elected, as did others to bowl a lot. Then I told you that we had a detachment of Portuguese military police on the base. Well, there was one fellow in particular that I kept running into around the island. He seemed to be at the bowling alley each time I was there. He didn't speak much English and I spoke very little Portuguese, but we had spoken at the main gate as I had entered the base now and then. I discovered later that he tried to be wherever I was.

One evening at the bowling alley, as I was making my way to the ladies room in the back of the building, he stepped out of the shadows and slipped his hand around my waist. He slowly drew me to him and kissed me. Now, I had taken some Karate classes. I was not a black belt, but had taken care of myself in more than one similar circumstance before. However, this time, I did not resist, in fact, to my surprise, I joined in the kiss. I did finally pull back, and muttered "olla". He smiled and so did I. No, I wasn't drunk and I wasn't sick. Somehow, it just felt comfortable. Then, I just muttered, rather breathless, "bye", stepped around him continuing on to the ladies room. He didn't resist my leaving, or follow me. He just stood there. When I came out, he was gone, and I returned to my bowling. I did look around for him, but he was no where to be found. I still saw him around the base from time to time, but we just smiled at each other, (like we had a secret) and went on our way. It was like a joke. I didn't give it any merit. But I did wonder why I was so casual about what had happened at the bowling alley.

About a week later, a friend of mine came up to me at the wives club and said that she had been seeing a local MP on the sly. She had over heard one of the young Portuguese MPs say that he had a crush on me. Excuse me, first I had to get over what she had said. I guess that I was sort of a local celebrity, and I had heard more than a few guys say that they were fans. I never took it seriously. Then I just laughed at her and said, "Right". When she convinced me that she was serious, I asked her to point out this fellow with such good taste. Still not taking this situation very much to heart. When we entered the base, she saw him, and you guessed it, it was the same fellow I had encountered the week before in the bowling alley. She said his name was Paulo.

Now as I have said, this was a very small island, and we were a tight community. I knew just about everyone stationed there, and I drove a pink Mercury which everyone also knew on sight. Why would I want to let anyone know how ignorant I was by committing adultery in front of the whole base. And most importantly, why would I want to?

I started to wish this fellow would get a huge transfer to another base. It prayed on my mind, so one afternoon I drove down to the beach to think. I was walking on the beach down by the ruins of the old fort where I had gone before to think. Yep, he was there, too. I walked around the corner of the old fort, and there he sat. We both laughed. He said that this was his thinking spot too.

We talked, mostly sign language, as we couldn't find a language that we could both speak fluently. He was from a small village near Lisbon, and had two more years to serve at this base. He was very nice and easy to talk too. Oh, he was very handsome, also. We strolled on the beach, and he came close and gently slipped his hand in mine as we strolled some more. I was not thinking too much as we sat on the rocks and watched the tide come in. He tried to tell me some old stories and tales of the island's history. I realized that I'd been there longer than planned, and he walked me to my car. As we reached my car, he asked if he could see me again. I said "Maybe", and he smiled and kissed me goodbye. We did meet again, quite a few times. We would drive into the village and shop, or up into the hills and watch the training of the bulls. There was a ranch in the hills for the raising and training of bulls for the arenas on the mainland. Or we'd check out the water caves. One afternoon we went up above the base and watched them practice the "Fulton recovery" which the Air Force was perfecting at that time. It is truly a sight to behold, kind of poetry in motion, so to speak. It is rather matter of fact these days, and is performed in a lot in military movies. It is a system of retrieval used by the military to pick up a person on the ground (or in the water) quickly and without the use of additional personnel.

The children really liked to go and watch them practice in the afternoons after school. We would take a picnic basket and a blanket and take turns doing a play by play of the action, like a sportscaster.

One afternoon I was doing some paper work in the scout hut, which was an old hanger that the Air Force had renovated for us. Paulo spotted the car and stopped to chat and more. Talk about a dose of reality! The thought of making love in the Scout hut really jolted me and set me to doing some serious soul searching. What was I thinking and was I even thinking about how stupid and really wrong the whole affair was for all of us; especially Dave. I had never lied to him before, and frankly, I was not good at it. I had gotten so caught up in the deception that I was a wreck. I tried not to see Paulo any more. I tried to change my schedule, so he wouldn't know where I was. I told him that we could not be alone ever again. I couldn't trust myself at all. I needed time to turn myself around. I couldn't believe that I was such a wimp about the whole thing. I was truly, and with good reason, hating myself. He said he understood and would stay away for, what seamed to be long periods of time, but when I'd least expected it, I would look up and there he would be. I started having nightmares about the whole situation. I felt guilty when I made love to my husband, like I was cheating on Paulo. That is so wrong!!!!!! Everything was wrong.

In order to figure out a way to get away from Paulo I told Dave that maybe I should go back to the states and wait for him to finish this tour. We could meet at the next base. He didn't see why. We were fine. He thought everything was going great. We decided I was suffering from island fever. He put in a request for our family to go on an R&R (rest and re-cooperation) to Germany for a couple of weeks, because just maybe I was going stir crazy. I had been on this island too long.

He was having trips every couple of weeks and he didn't feel as confined as I did.

The kids were all for a trip, so off we went to Bavaria, and toured the castles in the south of Germany. I'm pretty sure we saw every one, and all the monasteries too. It truly was a great idea. It was a fantastic vacation, we rented a car and drove from castle to castle; and military recreation center to military recreation center, for the whole two weeks. It was a totally awesome trip.

When we returned to Frankfurt airport to go back to the base. We found the airport and the hotel full of army troops that were going back to the states from war games in Europe. The hotel was full and the overflow of GIs was sleeping in the lobby, restaurant, halls, and some were camped outside of the building. They were literally all over the place.

The first night, we slept in the rental car. The next morning we found some friends that had a room and we all took turns showering and napping in their room. We drove off base for dinner, and had the airport lock our baggage in a holding area. When we got back to the airstrip after dinner, we returned the car and went directly to the plane.

As we started unpacking our suitcases back at the base, we realized that something was not right; our clothes were in the wrong bags. A couple of the bags had clothes and souvenirs that were not ours. So we got in touch with some of the others from the plane to see if they were having the same problem. They were. We took the things that were not ours to the base MP station, and we all traded back with each other. Then we determined what was missing, and figured out who had stolen our jewelry and jumbled our belongings.

We had locked all the bags in the same secure cage at the airport. We contacted the airport in Germany, and it seems that in the rush of so many people passing through the terminal, someone was robbing the passengers. They thought they wouldn't get caught since we wouldn't know about the theft until we were long gone.

We never retrieved our lost items, but a couple of the security guards went to jail for the thefts. It was the Air Force to the rescue. The Air Force is insured for just such a problem as this, so we all had lots of paperwork to fill out and submit.

My personal major problem was that I didn't want to leave my favorite jewelry on the island, so I took it with me. And you guessed it, that was what was stolen from me. It was jewelry that Dave had brought to me from all over the world, and was totally irreplaceable. And I did know that the Air Force replaces all lost or damaged goods at the rate of thirty two cents on the pound. I was devastated to say the least. I wasn't totally alone. The kid's souvenirs, from our vacation were gone too. " Holy cow", was pretty much all we could say. But they couldn't take away our incredible vacation memories.

The bitter sweet part of our return to the island was that Paulo was gone. I did not know where he went or when he left, but I did know that I would never mess up like that again.

Immediately, I set out to make up for the problem I had created. I so had a lot of people (and the lord) to ask for a new start. I gave more time to my family. and was truly more humbled by the experience.

Then just when I thought things were going well, another surprise. At the next squadron party, one of the young new airmen, told me that he wanted me to have his baby. He was drunk, and not too quiet with his request. Dave looked at me, winked, and I saw that he knew I could handle the situation. So he stepped aside to let me field this one. I promptly told his stunned wife to take him home and make him feel loved, I had plenty of man at my house to take care of. It drew a huge laugh by all of the people who had stopped what they were doing and sat watching with open mouth, waiting for whatever or whoever would make the next move. The tension in the room was eased. I knew that the old saying, "No one is indispensable", has much wisdom. But, I also knew that some people are so great to have around that you need to consider them indispensable. Now, I could return to the real me again. And gave myself to my husband, totally and completely as the preacher said, "till death do us part"

Chapter twelve:..Now that reminds me..

A couple of years ago, the local Art Museum hosted the Rodin exhibit. My son David and his daughter Charlee, had come to visit and we (Summer, Chloe and I) took them to the exhibit. Charlee was six years old, and Summer and Chloe were two years old. It was a really great afternoon. The girls were in their strollers. We started our tour of the exhibit at the gift shop, doesn't everyone? We got the girls blue squishy statues of the thinker. Chloe promptly tore off his head, and wanted David to fix it. It seamed like a lost cause, and for the remainder of the afternoon, we were the proud owners of a headless thinker.

When we got home we superglued the big blue guy. It is now eight years later and there are two whole squishy blue guys adorning the wine rack in the dining room.

Love that superglue!

Charlee was having fun pushing first one stroller and then the other. Trying to make sure that she gave each girl equal time. The girls were very excited that she was giving them so much attention. We were observing the works of Rodin, laughing, joking, and in general having a wonderful afternoon. We looked around and saw one of the guards walking slowly behind us from room to room. When he realized that we saw him, he came over and told us that Charlee couldn't push the strollers inside the museum. The thought of the managers of the museum, he said, was that she was too young for the responsibility. She didn't take to kindly to that statement, as you can imagine. David and I pushed both strollers as we walked away. About ten minutes later, the guard came back to tell us that we could not take pictures inside the Museum. He told us that he could confiscate our camera, but was feeling especially generous at the time. Well, this time he didn't leave, but followed us all the way to the door, saying from time to time not to touch the paintings or the statues.

He was holding the door for us to exit when the assistant curator came up to us. She said how proud she was that we were exposing our young ones to the culture of the museum. She went on to say that not enough people understand how a trip to the museum can develop a young child's appreciation of fine art. David and I just looked at each other and smirked. We had been vindicated. The guard was still holding the door for us to exit. We did not tell the assistant curator that her security guard was not as happy to see us visit as she was. I personally thought we were great visitors. We had fun too. We laughed all the way to the car.

A couple of weeks later, Austin, Tori, Gaye and I had a girl's night out. We went to the Rodin exhibit. Of course, during the tour, I had to point out where we were followed and how we were personally escorted out the door by the security guard. At the end of this tour we had our picture taken in front of the statue of the gates of hell. We tried to look wretched, as the guys in the statue, but we were laughing too hard.

The visit to the museum "reminded me" of another trip to a museum. That trip was to the Louve Museum in Paris. When we were stationed in Stuttgart, Germany, Tori and David took a French class at school. The end of the year was the class trip to Paris.

I was, at any given moment, on anything that had wheels and was going touring while we were in Europe. So when they asked me to be a chaperone, I was there. We were in Paris for a week, and took in all the sights that we could squeeze into a week. We walked the Chanceleze, climbed (took the elevator)up the Eiffel Tower, strolled along the left bank of the Seine, caught a show at the Moulin Rouge, stormed Notre Dame, checked out Rodin's workshop, and turned the world famous flea market upside down. Then we (the 40 teenagers and three chaperones) descended on the Louve Museum. One of our boys climbed up on the Winged Victory statue. A couple of our students went under the ropes that were protecting the Mona Lisa original painting and set off an alarm. We had our teenagers all over the building. I am surprised we didn't get deported that day.

I felt very faint, so I went to the restroom while the other chaperones rounded up our crew to head back to the hotel for dinner. I did not know that I was pregnant before we left Germany. I had been feeling a little under the weather on the whole bus ride, but didn't want to ruin everyone else's trip, so I didn't say much about it. I was feeling responsible for the class, as the French teacher had disappeared the same hour we checked into the hotel- to make a quick visit to some friends in Paris. I had some bad cramps by the time we got to the Louve, but was basically trying to keep our group out of jail. I could not wait any longer. I found the restrooms and the moment I got there, I felt the pressure in my abdomen. The blood flowed, I couldn't stop it and there wasn't any toilet paper. I did find some paper towels, and started to clean up as much as I could. I looked around and it looked like someone had been killed in there. The blood had splattered all over the bathroom. I had locked the door because I didn't want to be interrupted. The blood was caked all the way down to my knees.

It had rained off and on all day, and I had a long raincoat on. And I was wearing a dark blue pantsuit. So no one could see the blood. I was really feeling faint by this time, but I couldn't tell anyone about what had happened. I finally got everything cleaned as well as I could, and rushed everyone out of the museum. My final thought was that they would be looking for the body when the cleaning crew went into the bathroom.

We took the subway back to the hotel, and I washed out my clothes in the biday. I took a lot of vitamins, and aspirin and passed out. The next day we left on the bus. When we got back to the base in Germany, I immediately went to the base hospital. They performed a DandC.

The doctor said I'd had a miscarriage, with a few days rest and I would be fine. So, I told Dave and the kids the whole story after dinner that evening. That was my last pregnancy, but not my last visit to a museum.

*Chapter thirteen:..*Now That Reminds Me..

The other day, I received a letter in the mail, from my bank telling me of the perks that I could acquire if I added some new processes that they now have at my disposal. That, of course reminded me of the perks I had received as an Air Force wife. Dave was on flying status and was gone most of our marriage. He however always remembered me and the children with a small token of each trip. When the children were little, he would save some of his flight lunch (or dinner), like a pack of cookies or a roll of lifesavers for them.

Of course he always had a special gift for me. He always kidded and told me he was going to tie a ribbon around his waist and present himself to me. It was a private joke. What he did not know was that I was a more than willing recipient. So, I smiled coyly and giggled. When the children were tucked in bed, I would slip into the bathroom, shower and lotion head to toe, make a silent entrance into the bedroom clad in my birthday suit. I would pause at the light switch, salute, flip off the light, slip between the sheets and we would exchange special gifts. "I never did get that bow".

On Dave's first trip to the Philippines he decided to really surprise me with the most unusual gift he could think of. It worked. He brought me a hand carved set of utensils, a fork and a spoon. The surprise was that they were each five and a half feet tall. On the plane back to South Carolina the crew called the gift "Burk's folly". We all loved them, and they are still hanging in the alcove in the dining room. Over the years, they have been quite a conversation starter. When the grandchildren were little, I told them that they were grandpa's baby spoon and fork. I really didn't think they believed me.

When we were stationed in South Dakota, and California, Dave would have trips to Alaska. The crew would bring back King Crab on ice to us. I started collecting recipes for crab while we were on the west coast. Crab dip turned out to be my best dish.

When we were stationed in Germany, he'd bring us real Danish from Denmark and Oranges from Majorca. Once he found a bronze medallion with my astrological sign on it, at the flea market in Athens. The jewels he brought from Brazil were just the stones. I would have them set in a mounting that I designed with a local jeweler. It was very exciting. It was much less expensive that way.

When we were stationed in Europe and Dave had a trip back to the states, he brought us fresh bread and bags of potato chips. Once the bace exchange gave us another perk. The commander ordered us Christmas trees from the states. They were sent to us by boat. By the time we got the trees, they only had a few needles on them. But we loved them anyway, and just laughed about it. We took three trees and tied them together. The kids made ornaments of paper, so they wouldn't weigh down the trees. That was also the Christmas Dave brought us a movie camera back from his trip to Florida. It was great fun to play with. Dave would catch people coming into the house, and hit them with four hundred watts of lights, right in the kisser. From that new toy, we still have quite a few interesting home movies of normal friends with their faces all squinted and twisted. Of course, some of them are down right unrecognizable.

All in all I am so grateful. Being an Air Force wife, has given me some beautiful experiences, (perks) during the years. Where else could I have toured both the wine country sides of Germany's Rhine Valley and California's Napa Valley? How could I have seen the Mt. Rushmore statue, the Crazy Horse Statue, the Castles of Europe, the Roman ruins at Trier, the painted desert (at night, remember?), the grand canyon, the continental divide, the Aurora Borealis, the petrified forest of California, the Atlantic, the Pacific, the Gulf of Mexico, and so much more?

We witnessed one of the last remaining Mustang horse herds on the mesa in southern Colorado. What a breathtaking sight. The most amazing part of all of this, is that we took in and admired all of these great sites on what is considered a "below poverty level income". That is Dave's pay as an Air Force sergeant, along with the pay I brought in from jobs I found from time to time.

When we got to California the first time, we found out that we qualified for food stamps. What a shock to all of us, we thought we were just fine. Dave said it was ludicrous, and we turned them down.

Perks? Yes. I had the perks. I met two presidents on tour of Air Force bases during their tours in office. I met movie stars at golf tournaments and great singers entertaining the troops. I met people from around the world, and found them to be fun, outgoing and interested in other cultures as I was. They shared stories of their families and cultures.

There were times during our military service that we were able to get together with the neighbors two days before payday (we were all broke). Everyone brought what they had in the pantry, or fridge. We shared dinner, so we could all have a warm meal to hold us over (especially the children). I am aware that this doesn't sound like a perk, but the camaraderie, the closeness and dependency we all had was unforgettable. There were perks for the children during Dave's time in the military, also. We had access to some awesome birthday parties for the children. One year, we had a birthday party in the base skating rink. The rink was open just for the party for four hours. The kids were in charge of the program and the announcing for the party. Of course, there was an adult technician to aid them and to make sure there were no accidents. The kids had a great time being in charge (so to speak).

One year, we had a birthday party in the NCO Club, where the band that was performing (from England) for the month, offered to play for the party. We had bingo and popcorn for the kids also. Of course, there was a minimum fee. We had to set up the party decorations and clean up after, but in a civilian environment we never could have afforded to throw a party like that anywhere else.

There were the times when we changed bases in the middle of a tour. If we were already set up in base housing when Dave was reassigned, they would give us base housing when we reached the new base. Sometimes there were no Non Commissioned Officers quarters available, and to our pleasant surprise, we would be assigned officer housing. It was their version of an upgrade. That was too amazing to turn down. Chances were that we wouldn't be at that base for too long, but we always made the best of the situation.

There were some small drawbacks to this perk. As the lowest ranking man's wife, I got all of the jobs that no one else wanted. I had to call maintenance if there were any problems, and negotiate times for repairs. I had to collect and pay on time each month, the dues for the sector. If there were flowers to be sent to a family (for a death or birth), I had to arrange it. If any of the children were causing trouble, I had to report the incident to the Air Police. So, you get the idea. But, it surely was worth it. Living in upgraded quarters made the assignment more pleasant, that's for sure.

When we were stationed at a base in Germany near Mainz, we lived in the old compound where the "Panzer Division" had been stationed (the German's elite tank force, during world war II). It was located across the highway from where the USA crossed the Maine River and pushed the German army back to Berlin. Every year the town Mayor hung a wreath on the main gate in honor of the fallen German soldiers from the division.

We lived on the third floor of our building. The building had wide stairwells, and high ceilings (about twelve feet). The buildings had been renovated and turned into apartments for us. We had all three children in one bedroom, and there was still space for them to have a play area after their beds, dressers, night stands and toy boxes were brought in. Our bedroom looked like a football field, which made our double bed look like a postage stamp. Our apartment was so large, that the squadron always wanted us to host the parties. When the new families arrived at the base, they wanted to check out where we lived. Most of them thought it was a joke until they saw it. The only difficult part of living in the complex was when I returned from my bi-monthly visit to the commissary. I would park in front of the building, take the bags of groceries inside the building, then move them up to the second floor, the third floor, and then into the kitchen (which was at the far end of the apartment. The children always wanted to help, but they were five, six and seven at the time. Bringing in groceries was always an adventure. A funny part of this apartment to me was the fire escape outside our bedroom window. We were also pretty far from the base in this complex. To help with the everyday needs, a small grocery store was added in the basement of one of the buildings. It was truly a different experience living there. The attics still had the bullet holes all over the place, and our basement storage spaces had been holding cells for American soldiers that were captured during the fighting. The posters that were on the walls were from the soldiers that had been held there during the war. So, we left them up while we were there, to remind us of what had happened there twenty years before.

And the last and perhaps the greatest "perk" of all, was when Dave received the Distinguished Flying Cross, the Air Force's highest honor. I received a letter from the President of the United States, thanking me for my service to our country. You hardly ever hear of anyone thanking the wives or the families of our countries heroes. It was so special to me, to be thought of and to be made a part of my husband's service to our country, all I could do was sit there and cry.

Chapter fourteen:..Now that reminds me..

It is spring this week, and spring break is almost here. At this time of year, I find myself reminded of our family vacations over the years. We didn't have vacation money programmed into the budget, so we vacationed on our way from tour of duty to tour of duty.

The base changes almost always occurred during the summer months. Every now and then, we would have a move during the Christmas break. The vacation then would consist of a visit to a relative's home during the move. We could also stay, for a while, in the temporary quarters on base until we found a place to live. Or until on base housing became available. We drove to the new base whenever possible. We would act like tourists, and vacation as we were driving.

We would check the road signs, and make short side trips. One of our favorite side trips were the caverns that we found in quite a few states. They were a lot of fun, as well as educational.

We did take a side trip while in Texas one summer afternoon. The sign said, "This way to view the Texas long horn cattle". We set out to see the herd. It turned out to be one long horn steer, and his buffalo friend. That was a laugh.

We reached the Grand Canyon on a cold New Years Day, one year. It was ten degrees outside. Needless to say, we didn't take the donkey trip down into the canyon, but we got some great pictures of us shivering on the rim of the canyon.

As we were returning to the interstate to continue on to California, we saw a young man and woman standing by a broken down car on the side of the road. We stopped to see if they were OK. Our Volkswagen station wagon was packed with stuff that my mom had given us as we left her house. We had just come back to the states from Germany, and were on our way across the country to California. Our three kids were packed into the back seat. Still, maybe there was something we could do to help.

We discovered that it was their battery, and a jump start would not help. They were just married the day before and were on their way to their honeymoon when the car stopped.

We thought about phoning for help, but there were no phones in sight. This was the day before cell and on star. We took a quick vote and squeezed them into the back seat, (with the battery too). We took them to the nearest gas station where, luckily there was a mechanic to help them. We said a tearful goodbye and proceeded on to California.

I just have to throw this in. As California got closer, we saw signs saying that we could buy cactus before we crossed the border. We certainly had seen our share of cactus on this trip and it looked like we could use a plant to brighten our new home. A living souvenir, so to speak. So, we bought one, and put it in the back on top of the luggage.

When we reached the border between Arizona and California, the state patrol confiscated our beautiful cactus. He said that live vegetation could not be transported across state lines. We did notice that he had confiscated bags of oranges that day from tourists traveling from California to Arizona. We just couldn't believe it all. Then Dave said,

"At least the west to east tourists could have stopped just short of the border and had a picnic. We would have had to flip a coin to see who eats the "cactus".

One of our short weekend trips, while we were stationed in California, was into the northern part of the state. We were looking for the Petrified Forest. I had a brochure from the NCO club saying it was a great attraction, and very educational for the children. It was a longer drive than we expected, so after I had napped a bit, I offered to drive so Dave could get a nap also, and be ready for all of the hiking we would do when we reached the forest. I was driving along, when I saw an unexpected sign. I turned off the highway and while everyone was asleep, I drove into (inside) a giant redwood tree. I stopped the car and woke everyone up. What a look on everyone's face. Now, that was cool.

One Christmas, we went from Florida to South Dakota. We stopped in Ohio to spend the holidays with family and friends. We bought some warm clothes, and continued on our way. Unfortunately the car froze up as we were driving one night in the great state of Iowa. We had some blankets in the car, so we wrapped the kids up in them. Dave's strategy was to let the car rest a few minutes, and then start it again. It would go a few miles, and it would die again. There were miles and miles of miles and miles. We nursed the engine along a very lonely stretch of road.

Finally in the distance we saw lights from a town. It was touch and go for a while, but we made it. We made it to a gas station and asked them what we could do to make it to South Dakota. They installed an engine heater and we continued on with no problems. When we got there, we plugged in our car each night during the rest of the winter. Yep, we just pulled the car up to the back door, and plugged it in to keep the engine from freezing over night.

One night, we did the usual-plug in the car, and went to sleep. Well, before morning we had a turn in the weather, and everything thawed. So, that in the morning, the back yard was completely mud. When we tried to get the car out of the yard, it sunk further in the mud. We dug out the tires and put wooden planks under the tires all the way to the street. We got the car out by noon. But we sure tore up the yard in the process.

By the time we moved to the Rocky Mountains, in Colorado, we had the,-plug in the car-routine down pat. It became automatic to listen to the weather just before turning in for the evening, to see if you should plug in or not.

When we were transferred to California it was a pleasant surprise. My brother and his family were living in San Jose, just south of San Francisco. We were stationed just north of San Francisco, in San Raphael. One weekend a month one family would drive to visit the other, and the next month we would reverse the drive. It became a contest as to who could have the best sight seeing trip planned for the weekend that we were the host family. After a year had passed, we tallied the weekend visits. John's family won hands down for the best host and hostess. They had taken us to the Warf, the audience participation theater, the Chinese New Year Parade, the chocolate factory, two wine tours, the trolley car ride, and Lombard Street. Our sight seeing trips included, the static display of the airplanes on base, with the fly over by the Thunderbirds, the California petrified forest (it has two trees), a picnic in the mountains (where it snowed as we tried to eat), a wine tour in Napa valley, a fancy dinner at the NCO Club on base followed by bingo, and the trip up the coastal highway to Big Sir (where the traffic was unbelievable).

Yep, they won, hands down.

We tried a lot of new things in California. We started recycling while we were there. We got hooked on pastrami and swiss sandwiches, as well as other deli treats. We started drinking bottled water while we were there. We took turns babysitting each others children so we could have a second honey-moon.(we really never had the time for a first honeymoon, but who was counting). It was a great tour of duty for all of us. Soon after the celebration, Dave got sent to Viet Nam for another unaccompanied tour.(that meant that the kids and I were not allowed to go).   Dave was promised the base of his choice when he returned to the states. He took the kids and I to Florida. He put in for Florida before he left the base to serve his tour in Thailand. He would meet us there. And sure enough, he met us there. He was there just long enough to get transferred to South Dakota.

That was not the south he had in mind. And it was winter. So we stopped at my mom's house and filled the suitcases with winter clothes. My grandmother gave me a coat that her son had worn in the Forties when he went to South Dakota. She also told me that when I would have to go to the barn, I should wear the coat and tie a string from the back door to the barn, because that is how you find things in a whiteout. Needless to say, by the time I got there I was a little bit nervous.

She was pretty close to right about some things. I wore that coat a lot, and was glad to have it. White outs were disastrous. People got lost and froze just steps from their homes. We lived on base, so we were OK.

The way the base to base transfer worked was that in the States you could be transferred from base to base. But when your tour of duty in a foreign country was over, you had to return to a stateside base. So, driving to the next base in Europe was not an option. If we wanted to vacation, or see the sights, we had to do it while we were stationed there. When Dave had a few days between flights, and had caught up on his paperwork, we could often take a long weekend to travel around the area.

The countries in Europe are like the states. They are very close, and when you are in Germany, you can drive to quite a few other countries on the weekend. We would get out the map, and pick a destination for our short tour. I was not concentrating on the map on one such outing. When Dave asked me where we were on the map, I looked down and realized that we had driven off the map. We were somewhere in northern Belgium. We had just passed a soccer stadium. They were in the process of a game. Because soccer is a very emotional sport, and the game was obviously very good, (the fans were going crazy). We elected not to stop and ask for directions. We decided to backtrack until we found the little eatery we had stopped at short time before. We turned around and proceeded on to find ourselves realizing that we weren't paying that much attention to exactly where we were going, just enjoying the countryside and counting cows.

All of a sudden, David (my son) leaned forward in the seat, as if to ask a question. I started to turn around, but before I could, he had thrown up down the back of my neck, and all over himself. We pulled off the road a ways, and got some paper towels out of the back of the car. Cleaning us up as best we could, it was decided to finish the job when we returned to the eatery.

This is a great place to tell you about the eatery. It was a beautiful quaint little place. What we call a mom and pop operation. Traveling, as we did, we found the people to be so friendly, and warm. When they found out we were Americans, they could not help us enough. They wanted to find out as much as they could about the states. They also wanted to practice their English. Most of them spoke English with an English accent, it was so funny. The fellow that owned the eatery wanted to know how we liked the food in Europe. We told him the kids favorite foods were hamburgers and fries. So he said OK and went into the kitchen. We talked with his wife and the other customers while we waited for the food. One of the waiters pulled out a mandolin and played while we talked. It was a very pleasant afternoon.

When the food came to the table, we all looked down and then we looked at each other. They had brought us a lot of food. Enough to feed us for a couple of days. But the most surprising part was that the hamburger was lying there on the bun uncooked. We didn't want to offend these nice people, but we sure didn't want to eat this raw hamburger meat either. The kids and I started on the rest of the food, which was very good, while Dave went into the kitchen. He very tactfully explained to our host that the meat needed to be cooked. He was really good at those things. The man apologized and cooked the hamburgers for us. All in all, a good time was had by all.

With a little maneuvering we made our way back to the map. When anyone of us saw a landmark they remembered from before, they would call out and we would head that way. It worked and we got back to the base safe and sound, even if we were a little smelly.

After this adventure, I was known as the wayward navigator. We still got lost from time to time, but we all made sure that we never drove off the map again.

There was a vacation that the children and I took without Dave. We were at a base in South Dakota when Dave got assigned to Europe again. He went ahead, and we (the kids and I) took care of the moving details. I really didn't think we'd be back to South Dakota. After we got our possessions packed and before we left the state, I wanted to go to Yellowstone National Park. There were only a couple of days until we had to be in New Jersey. Everything had to work like clockwork. We had sold our car to a fellow on base. It was in the bill of sale that we could drive until we left the base. After packing the car full of blankets, pillows and food, the four of us headed over to the Park. It was totally awesome. When we got to the entrance of the park, there was no ranger to greet us. There were no signs saying it was closed, so we entered the park. As we pulled into the park, we came upon a female moose and her baby. They were as surprised as we were. We looked at them, they looked at us. I was completely speechless. The kids just kept smiling. They moved on past the car slowly, and disappeared into the forest.

I was so glad that we had made the trip. The bubbling hot springs were cool, and the Geyser really does erupt on schedule. We found a campground in the evening and sat around a campfire with some other visitors to the park. David had gone to the bathroom a ways up the slope, and came back dragging something that looked like a bear trap. That was because it was a bear trap. He wanted to take it home. I remembered the last time we were in a national park and had picked up some pinecones to take as souvenirs. We had to backtrack from the gate and put them back in their original place. I didn't want to do that again, so we left the trap by the campfire (unset). It was very cold that night, and we slept in the car wrapped up in our blankets. We kept thinking a hotel would be great, but unfortunately, we didn't have the money for one. The next day, we drove around looking for more wildlife. We didn't find any, but it started to snow, so we headed back to the base, gave up the car, got our luggage, signed out of the quarters, and boarded a plane for New Jersey. Ahead of us was another new adventure.

I really loved the excitement and the day to day challenge of being an Air Force wife. I was so determined to make our marriage a success, as year after year I saw how many didn't last. Especially for the guys that were on flying status. We sat down and figured out that Dave had been TDY (temporary duty) or on missions for a little over half of our married life. We had it worked out so that when Dave was gone, I took charge of the household, and when he was home, he took charge. It worked out, as each of us felt like a full partner.

Our first base together was Donaldson AFB in South Carolina. One March, we got assigned to Wiesbaden, Germany. That was the year that the Rhine River froze over, and also the first time that the base we had just left was closed. This was the beginning of the "Legend of Carol" as our families called it. We closed a good many bases and lived through a good many natural disasters throughout the years between 1956 and 1978. It became a huge joke at family reunions.

Chapter fifteen:..Now That Reminds Me..

When the dog barks early in the morning, I know the neighborhood children are out in front waiting on the school bus. It is curious, because we have to drive our little ones downtown to their school, and the kids from down the block and the kids from one street over catch their bus in front of our house. I guess somehow, somewhere, it all balances itself out.

As I check on the kids, out in front, it reminds me of when I returned to school at the ripe old age of fifty three. When Dave died, I was devastated. We had a pact to grow old together. He broke that pact. He bailed on me. How could he?

The Chaplin told me there are many stages that face the living after the funeral. I was not sure which one I was in when Gaye told me I should go to College. There was a Community College just down the road from us that would give me a new start. At first, I just dismissed the idea. I thought she must be crazy. I had been out of school for thirty five years. She didn't give up on me and finally I tried it. She encouraged me to talk to a counselor. Zach told me that he would help me with my homework. So, I made an appointment with a counselor at the college. She was very helpful and also encouraging.

We worked out a plan where I would go to the college library twice a week and pretest to see how much "book learning" I had retained. We would check the scores, and the instructor would give me some more refresher materials. I went back twice a week for two months to study and ask questions. She helped me pick out a class schedule, got me the paperwork for financial help, then I retested. I was impressed with how well I did on the retest. I took the entrance exam with all those young "whipper snappers". I was the oldest student at the college, at the time, and they referred to me as their new and nontraditional student. I was there for two and a half years, and was very often mistaken for a teacher.

About the time I graduated, most of the students and teachers had gotten used to me in the halls. I got a part time job working for one of the professors a couple of hours a day, between my classes.

All in all, it was really an incredible experience. I will always be glad, I did it. During those two years, I was a member of two sororities. I was named in the "Best College Students of America Yearbook" which made me very proud of myself. Of course I had the help and support of my children and grandchildren. I know that I couldn't have done it alone. But there were those that said it couldn't be done at all......... and I had done it!!!!!!

*Chapter sixteen:..*Now That Reminds Me..

In an earlier chapter, I told you about the "legend of Carol". On the evening news today, there was a story and pictures of a line of tornados that tore thru a small town in the west. That reminded me of the mother nature's surprises our family has lived thru over the years. Let's see, there were the not one, but two dams collapsing in two separate states.

We were there.

The first one was in South Dakota when our children were teenagers. One spring after the big thaw in the mountains, a dam burst and sent a twenty foot wall of water roaring into town. The results were devastating to the town and the base. The water leveled a path thru the heart of town. By the time it got to the base, there was flooding, but most of the fight was gone from the torrent of water.

The people on the base took in the town's people until they could go to live with relatives, or get things back to normal. We collected food and clothing, distributed them to those in need, as well as volunteered where we could be of the most use.

The second dam break we were witness to was in Colorado some years later. One summer morning, a dam in the mountains collapsed and sent a surge of water that rushed into a lower dam. The force of it, broke that dam. The combined waters then headed into the middle of town. It seams that when the town was settled, the founding fathers changed the flow of the river that had run thru the town. Well, the surge of water that entered town on that summer morning took the original route. This was the height of the tourist season, so there were a lot of campers in the mountains, and a lot of tourists in town.

We had a gift shop on the main street of town, and a house overlooking the main street. We started the short hike to the shop that morning. As we got to the crest of the hill and looked down onto the street, we stopped abruptly and were speechless. There was no street, no stores, and no shop. All we saw was water rushing like rapids below us. We couldn't tell how deep it was. It just looked like rapids with wood, and rocks churning around down the center of town. It was early in the morning, so the main street had been deserted. There was no way of knowing how many people had been hurt or killed at that point. There was no way of knowing how far down the mountains the damage continued.

We were stranded up there, on the mountain. All roads were unusable, phone lines were down, and the people that had left town before the break, couldn't get back. (Our oldest daughter, Gaye, was one of those people) We were cut off from the outside world until they realized what had happened down the mountain. About noon they sent some helicopters to check us out. It took a year to clean up and rebuild. The press called it a miracle that we got things back in place that quickly.

One of the things that helped us was, that we (my husband, I and another couple that owned a gift shop in town) salvaged the merchandise that we could, went to Denver and bought more merchandise. We combined all this and went to the other side of the mountains (west slopes) to open a shop for the winter season. That enabled us to get some capital for the next summer. We had to find a way to subsidize the next summer, as none of us had flood insurance. Our insurance agent said flood insurance was only available in the flood plane area. There was a city map showing no flood plain in the heart of town. We were not in a flood plain officially. And as such, we didn't have flood insurance.

When the water receded, we were left with three feet of mud to dig out. The citizens got together and tried to find a way to save our businesses. In the process, we hired lawyers to defend our position. The insurance companies claimed it was the governments fault, the state government claimed it was the federal governments fault and vice versa. The case passed from agency to agency, and then ten years later, we got a check from the court for one thousand dollars as our share of the loss from the flood, minus our lawyer fees. As you can imagine, that was not anywhere near the cost of the building and merchandise that we had lost. We had all just bought merchandise for the summer and of course lost almost all of it in the flood. We just kept going, because if we had stopped, we would all fall down.

The number of bases that closed while we were stationed there grew as the years passed. There was the base in South Carolina first, and one in Florida. The next one was in Germany. When we left the base in California, they closed it too. Here we go again. All we did was visit the base in France, and the next month the government gave it to the French. They left everything there but the men. They even left the silverware and the sheets.

When we came back to the states, the government kept saying they were going to close the base in North Carolina, but it is still operating to this day.

Perhaps the "Legend of Carol" has done an about face, finally...

Chapter seventeen:..Now that reminds me..

When it rains hard and the wind blows, I love to watch it. I find it very fascinating. When Zach and Austin were little, we turned our garage into a work shop/playroom for them. The young'uns and I would open the garage door, pull up some lawn chairs, and eat our popcorn while watching the wind whistle by and the rain fall on the front lawn on a lazy afternoon. I would tell them stories of their parents as children and teenagers.

As we watched the rain, they would ask for one of their favorite stories about the first time we moved to Florida. The story goes: When we got to the base, we didn't have a place to live yet, so we stayed in the guest quarters for a while. The first thing we saw as we approached the quarters was the hurricane warnings and policies posted on the front door. The windows were taped and a reminder was there on the tape that we were now in a favorite spot for hurricanes that came out of the Gulf of Mexico. In fact, the locals call it "Hurricane Alley". That was a very sobering thought.

After we moved into base housing a savage hurricane struck the coast just south of the base. We didn't get much sleep that night. Finally by early morning it seemed to be gone, so we all got ready as usual. Dave went to the flight line, the kids went off to school (the school was on base) and I started off to my job in town at a department store.

I didn't even get a block off base and I began seeing the destruction. When I finally reached the corner where the store was, it was not there any longer. It was gone. Completely gone. It turned out that the eye of the storm had landed on the coast just south of the base. It had gone north about a block before the main gate of the base and taken a sharp left turn. When I got myself together, I made my way back to the base. By then, they all knew about the devastation that was just down the road.

We, the airmen and families set out to help the people that had been caught in the path of the storm. We volunteered clothes, food, people to clean up and rebuild. I got so busy volunteering I could not work.

The town did recover, but they never rebuilt the store where I had worked. It turned out to be the start of my, as Dave called it, professional volunteer career.

Shortly after the hurricane struck, we were transferred to a new base. We began to move frequently from that point on. Quite often it was every year, and just as often to different countries. It was difficult for a military wife to get a job in those days. Mostly people wanted someone with more staying power. At foreign bases, the jobs were held by the nationals of that country. I spoke very little of any language except English. I made sure I could count and ask a few questions (learned from my children who took well to the local languages) I never was fluent in any of the languages before it was time to move.

Chapter eighteen:..Now That Reminds Me..

Last week, I caught my first cold of the season. I have been lucky the last few years, and haven't had too many colds and no flu. I am probably jinxing my health for the remainder of the year. What I am trying to get at is, that I haven't needed the usual amount of drugs for the past few years. During the late sixties and early seventies that was not the case. I was, what is now, in retrospect, referred to as a suburban junkie. I was a very young mother of three. My husband was gone most of the time, and in harms way, at the same time. Yes, I realized how dangerous his job was, but that didn't lessen the stress. I had a very sunny exterior, and a very terrified interior. I was determined not to appear to the world as a whinny wimp. I had to be extra strong for all of us. Family, friends and most of all for myself.

Well, as time marched on, keeping it all inside, as they say, took its toll on me. I developed migraines, and then rashes (that got so bad, my hands would break open and bleed). Upon visiting the clinics, they would give me a shot to calm down my nerves, or pills as a temporary measure. Quite often, I would have one pill on top of another. I didn't have the internet to look up all of the medication that I would be taking at any one time. Thinking that the doctors knew what they were doing, I just took them all. The thing that I should have thought about is that each time I went to the clinic, there was a different doctor working. Also, we changed bases quite often and our records didn't always get to the new base before we were on our way again. I thought I was fine. There were days and weeks at a time when I didn't remember what I had done the day before.

My friends never knew that I wasn't OK. I was a pillar of the community, and always there for everyone. At one point, we were transferred back to Europe, and Dave said it was lucky that we didn't have to pass through customs, or I would have been arrested for all the drugs that were in my train case.

The doctors had been treating the results instead of the cause, and after all the medication that I had taken, my blood pressure was out of sight. As you might have guessed, they gave me more medicine for that condition. I laughed because all those pills were prescriptions. I was sure it was OK.

When I was doing my radio show on Armed Forces Radio, a story came over on the ticker tape that I got each day from the states. It was about a housewife in California that had the same basic circumstances in her life that I had. The press called her a suburban housewife junkie. What a shock to my little system. That was me! Well, I fixed that quickly and quietly. I flushed every pill in my medicine cabinet down the commode. I vowed then and there only to take vitamins and an occasional aspirin. I am amazed that my system didn't go into shock, when I took away all those pills. Especially when I looked into the medication and saw what I had been taking. I was not an alcoholic, however I did have a drink from time to time, while taking all the medicine. Upon further investigation, I saw at one point I was taking four different hallucinatory drugs. I sure was calm, for that period of time.

I was so anti pill after that, when I was in a wreck with a semi truck (the truck fell on my car as I waited at a stop light) I wouldn't take any pain pills. Maybe, that was a little radical. Cause it sure was painful as they were sewing up my head and arm, and for quite a while after that. But, I held my ground and slowly the pain subsided. There were days when I gritted my teeth, while refusing the pills. I was so terrified that if I took the pain pills, I would become addicted to them. The hospital staff thought I was crazy. I was not ready to admit to anyone that I had been a housewife junkie. I certainly was not about to tell them why I would not take the medication, at that point. Aspirin became helpful at those times. I was very thankful.

From time to time I walk into a pharmacy and check my blood pressure. I find the blood pressure cuff, sit down, slip it on, push the button and feel the cuff tighten, and tighten, and tighten. As I wait for the results, there is a pang of fear. So far it has registered my blood pressure as a little high, but not out of control. And hopefully it will never get "out of control" again.

*Chapter nineteen:..*Now That Reminds Me..

A friend asked me the other day, how I was feeling. I replied, "fine". She acted like she didn't believe me. Not even acid reflux, she asked? "No", I replied. I have always been, as they say, healthy as a horse. So, that reminded me, that while I have been the picture of health, I have had my share of bumps and bruises over the years.

We were stationed at a base in Europe where there were stables. A friend of Dave's had bought a horse for his teen age daughter. They were being reassigned back to the states. Dave bought the horse for our children, so they would feel that Benecca would be loved and well cared for. The stable fee (which included grooming and feeding) was only seventeen dollars a month. We felt that we could afford it and we could get lessons for our little ones. There was a small catch with the horse. She wouldn't take a saddle. We visited the stable so the kids could get to know the horse, and visa versa. I decided to learn how to ride bareback, so I could show the kids how easy it would be. I got on the horse with the help of the stable attendant, and rode off the base. We had a nice easy ride, and we were both feeling compatible.

Then I made the mistake of saying to her, "OK girl, let's go home." She took off like a shot, and went straight toward the stable. I held on as tight as I could. As we neared the paddock, she made a straight line to her stall. But there was a fence around that area. OK, she jumped the fence, very smoothly. She went straight, and I flew to the left. I landed on top of the cement roller that had been used by the grounds keeper to level the paddock. I looked up into the sun, and a shadow crossed between us. It was the grounds keeper, shouting "don't move"! I remember thinking that was silly, I couldn't if I wanted to. The ambulance took me to the emergency room. I had cracked some ribs and broken my pelvis on the cement roller.

The doctor smiled and simply told me that I was too old to ride bareback. My thigh muscles weren't what the they had been in my youth. So as I was healing, Dave found a good home for Benecca. The new little girl owner, let the kids visit Benecca from time to time. And they were fine with that.

You know about the truck falling on my car as I was waiting for the light to change. You know about the miscarriage in the Louve, so let's move on.

There was the time I decided the trailer we lived in was dirty and proceeded to wash it the same way you wash a car. Why not, I thought. I took one of the bar stools we had and a mop outside anxious to get the job done. I balanced on the bar stool seat ready to make that aluminum siding shine. The ground was a little uneven. When I reached for that last bit of grime in the corner at the top, I went crashing down on to the leg of the metal chair and cracked both shins. Talk about not too bright.

Then there was the time in high school, after a driving class. I forgot my scarf in the back window of the practice car. I opened up the back door, grabbed the scarf, and promptly closed the door. I had forgotten to move my right hand first. As a result the door closed on my thumb. I tugged, but it was wedged in there really well. When they got my finger out of the closed door, I slipped to the ground. Out like a light.

So, I got carried into school by my teacher, as the rest of the class trailed in behind. And, you might have guessed, the bell between classes had just rung. The halls were full of kids. I experienced total embarrassment on that long hall to the nurse's office.

One night Dave and I went to an NCO picnic in a friend's truck. He had just built a camper on the back but had not yet installed lights. We had a few drinks, and danced away the evening (we even won a trophy for a dance contest). When we all left the picnic, Dave and I climbed into the camper. I stumbled and broke my foot. They wanted to take me to the emergency room, but I waited until the next day. So I could sober up first.

Then there was the day we went to the lake with a friend who had just bought a boat and a set of skis. I didn't know how to swim, even though Dave, who was a champion swimmer had tried to teach me. I was, and still am the one that sinks like a rock. He taught me how to dive one summer. When I dove into the water he was there to take me to the side of the pool. He thought he could teach me how to water ski. After all, we had life jackets. You know that when one of the group is learning how to ski, all the others have to give their piece of advice. Bend your knees, hold your arms straight, wave if you need to go faster, yell if you want to stop or slow down, and last but most important, when you fall (not if) let go of the rope and we will come back around for you. You have a life jacket on so you will float until we get back. OK, it is all swimming around in my head. I took off from the dock and it was very smooth, I kept the tips of the skis up and then leveled off. Wow, I was a natural. Right up until the turn that is. I lost my footing and, you guessed it, I forgot to let go of the rope. I kept saying it in my head as the boat pulled me through the water. The others were talking to each other in the boat and didn't see me fall. When they noticed that I was out of sight, they assumed that I had let go of the rope. So they turned to come back for me. Finally, Dave noticed that I was still holding on to the rope, and yelled at the driver to stop so they could pull me into the boat.

Well, you know that I didn't drown that day, but I also never water-skied again. I left it up to the champs, like Dave. But I can't, continue without telling you a story about him and his water-skiing. He worked really hard one summer, and became a top competitor in the Slalom skiing event at a local lake. The new exit from the water he came up with was very crowd pleasing. He would be pulled in a half circle close to the shore of the lake in front of the crowd, release the rope, slowly sink on the one ski and come to a stop on the shore. Well, one day he released early, and sank too far out from the shore. His ski stopped abruptly and he kept on traveling. He kept his wits about him, rolled onto the beach, jumped up with arms raised and did a loud "Ta-Da"! To which our three little ones jumped up and yelled, "Yea daddy, do it again". The crowd roared with laughter. I was picking sand out of his back for about a week after that. He was a pretty good sport about it. (right)

And as you guessed, here is another one of my incidents. I was working in the garden one fall weekend and was bitten by a spider. I didn't think too much about it, put some ice on it to ease some of the swelling. It didn't stop the swelling. About three days later it was huge as well as black and blue. What gave me cause for concern, were the red streaks that had started to come from the area. So on the way home from work, I stopped at a local emergency room. I told them I was bitten by a spider in the garden and when the doctor took a look at it, he told the nurse to get the operating room ready quickly. He explained that I had been bitten by a brown recluse spider. And the arm needed to be opened ASAP. So he numbed the area, but did not put me out. So I watched as he lanced my arm.

He was informing me on the habits of the brown recluse as he worked. This spider is different from the others in the way that it bites. It chews and leaves a venom that kills tissue. It rarely kills a person, but can kill animals as big as a horse. All the tissue that has poison in it must be scraped out of the wound. And the wound must heal from the inside out, so the wound has to be packed and scraped everyday until it heals. He shared a couple more gory stories, and was finished for the day. I drove home that day thinking of how to tell my family what had happened. Why I was a couple of hours late. It took four months for my arm to heal. After work I would drive forty five minutes to the base hospital to be unpacked, scraped, and repacked with iodized gauze. I was very lucky, the bite was very close to my heart, and the doctors were amazed that I didn't die. They liked showing my arm to all the staff as it healed, saying that I was a textbook case. I had to go back every evening on my way home for four months, so he could scrape the wound and repack it with iodized gauze. We had a lot of time to chat, and one evening I asked if I would be immune to further bites. Needless to say I was wishing for a "yes". But I got a "no". I was a little nervous about working in the garden for a while.

A few years before the spider incident, I was trimming the bushes in front of the house, and was taking a break to wipe my forehead when I discovered a small tick at my hairline. I went into the house, removed and disposed of it. I didn't give it any further thought. We were living at the outskirts of town, and very often had deer in the yard. So we were used to checking for ticks on a regular basis.

A few days later, I thought I had the flu, and went to the base hospital to get checked out. It was on a Saturday morning and there was a civilian doctor working in the clinic. She was fulfilling a national guard obligation. I told her my symptoms and she took a look at the bottoms of my feet. OK, she was a civilian, and from Duke University Hospital, so I thought it might be a new exam procedure. Or she was crazy. Then she asked if I had been bitten by a tick. I told her of the one that I had found a couple of days earlier, and she checked the spot on my forehead. Her diagnosis was Rocky Mountain Spotted Tick Fever. Now that is mouthful, and it scared me to death right there in the clinic. She said it was curable, but it might leave me with some knee problems. She gave me some mega doses of tetracycline. The Medicine made me so sick. I worried that I couldn't hold down enough to get rid of the tick fever. I did finally keep down enough to get rid of it, but it has left my knees a bit messed up.

And that reminds me of the other time I was packed with the iodized gauze for months. At a base dentist visit, in Germany, I had a full face x-ray. My first encounter with the procedure disclosed that I needed braces (which they gave me that very day), and also found a suspicious area in my jawbone. They checked it out and determined it was a tumor in my jaw bone. They kept an eye on the spot, waiting to see if it would grow. It was the consensus of the dental staff that it must be removed, so that is what they did. I was given a local anesthetic and the dental surgeon proceeded to operate. I had virtually no idea what he was doing, but I quickly saw what he was doing. I watched the operation in his glasses.

When he was finished removing the bone that held the tumor, he told me that I must return twice a week to have the area cleaned out and repacked with the iodine gauze. The doctor was a German dentist assigned to an army group that occupied an abandoned German fort. It was a very ominous looking place. It was also on the outskirts of town. I had to take the bus to the end of the line and walk another seven blocks. Then when he finished taking the X-rays and refilling my jaw with the iodized gauze, I would walk back to the bus stop and catch the bus back to the base housing. I laughingly called the doctor a mad scientist, and said he was writing a paper on regrowing bones. I guess I should have been scared, but I was in too much pain to even think that much. Well, he must have done something right, because the piece of jawbone he had removed regrew and is just as strong as before. Whatever he did left no scars and now I have a jawbone with no suspicious spots on it.

Just a couple more stories for you in this chapter. It was a Wednesday afternoon and I was on my way to choir practice. I was going a little too fast down the stairs here at home, and caught my heel on the third step. I fell down the fourteen steps bouncing twice and came to a sitting stop at the bottom of the stairs. I was in a bit of shock. Gaye came running in from her office, and asked if I was OK. I literally couldn't talk. I couldn't even breathe. I just sat there looking up at her. Zach had just gone out of the house, and came back in asking what that noise was. They called 911 and the ambulance was here in about five minutes.

I was still sitting there when they arrived. I had, however finally caught my breath a little. It was like one of those funny videos on TV. But, this one hurt. They gave me some oxygen, and talked to Gaye and Zach. Gaye called Tori and she met us at the hospital. The 911 guys wanted to take me in the ambulance, but I talked Gaye into taking me in her car. It was such a keystone cop's situation, I was sitting on the bottom step, sucking Oxygen, and the others were talking about me and my condition and what treatment I needed as if I weren't in the room. I got checked out at the hospital, just a few cracked ribs, some bruises and I needed some rest. They sent me home to re-coop. Which I did.

During one of our visits to my mom's house between bases, we had a scare. One evening we (Gaye, David, Tori, my mom and me) went to bed as usual. I had a terrible headache for no apparent reason. My dad and my brother came in from working late that evening. Tori,who was three at the time, woke up and began to cry. The guys heard her from downstairs. I had never let her cry for a long time. They waited for a few minutes but she didn't stop, and I was not responding to her. They went up the stairs, expecting to see me at her bed. When they tried to wake me, there was no response.

They thought they faintly smelled gas. They immediately opened all the windows and called the rescue squad. We were taken to the hospital after they revived us. We spent the rest of the night at the hospital to make sure that we were going to be OK. After being released from the hospital we spent the next couple of days at a friend's house. They discovered that the chimney was the culprit. It seamed that a couple of bricks had fallen inside of the chimney and clogged the air flow. The carbon monoxide was coming back into the house. It took the contractor two days to fix the chimney and air out the house. It turned out that Tori had saved our lives. And now she saves lives for a living as a Paramedic (Lt). We are all very grateful to her for being there when we need her to this day.

The doctor contacted the Red Cross to let Dave know we were going to be OK. If he found out about us being in the hospital he would go ballistic. They gave him a short leave to come and make sure we were OK., then we went back to Germany with him. That tour was a fairly quiet one, and we were glad.

I mentioned the truck fight before, but didn't give you the details. I was taking Gaye to work one afternoon, and Austin was asleep, so Dave stayed home while I took her. We were sitting at a stop light, talking and when I looked up, one of those grocery store diesel trucks was coming into the intersection from our left a little too fast, trying to catch the light before it changed. Then he realized this intersection was his right turn. He didn't slow down, he just turned. His truck was loaded with food he was delivering to the coast. The turn was so sharp and fast that the truck raised up off the pavement and came in our direction on it's side. It all happened so fast, that there was no time to think.

I just automatically tried to slip the car into reverse. There were three cars behind me, so that move was futile, but I tried anyway. Gaye grabbed me and pulled me as low as she could, before the cab of the huge truck landed on top of our car. The cab landed on top of us, and the trailer landed on the car in front of us.

About a half a mile from the intersection was a fire station, and the ambulance arrived on the scene in a couple of minutes. They pulled us out of the car, and we sat down on the side of the road for a minute. About the only thing I remember is that I looked down at my arm and thought, "wow the bones really are white". They rushed me to the base hospital. Gaye was badly bruised, almost all of her body. My left arm was a mess and I had cuts on my head that needed to be sewed up. They told me that I would not be able to use my left arm again. (I just want to tell you, at this point, I am typing this with both hands.)

The most bizarre part of the accident was when Dave took me to see the car. It really looked like a truck had fallen on it. The rear view mirror had been propelled into the car seat in the middle of the back seat. We had been told that was the safest place for a child's car seat.

We were so thankful that Austin had been asleep and had not gone with us that day. And that Zach was at school.

I surely don't want you to think that I am clumsy at all, but I have had some silly falls. Quite a few years ago, in the apartment complex pool, I was doing my bi-weekly water exercises (in the shallow end, 'cause I still cannot swim). I went up the steps to get the ball that had blown out of the pool onto the patio. But, when I went back down the steps, I stepped on a slick spot and went down on to the cement steps and hit my back very hard. I broke two ribs on that fall.

The x-ray tech said he thought I'd hurt my spine also, but on further examination of the x-rays, he discovered that my spine isn't straight, so it was spared. Now that is not a thing you hear often. So where is it? He showed me the x-ray, and it is off to the left of where it should normally be located. He was surprised that I can stand up. How about that?

After three children, two miscarriages, and six DandC's, the wall of my uterus collapsed. Parts of my bladder and bowel fell into it. I had no idea what was happening so off to the doctor I went. He explained what had taken place inside. With surgery, the problem could be fixed. The solution would be two fold. First, would be the repair of my bladder and bowel. Second, would be the removal of all the pink parts of the diagram he had just shown me.(a diagram of the female organs) It just so happened that the whole diagram was pink. Now you've got to love a doctor with a sense of humor. It would take about a week to set-up the surgery. OK, so be it. He put in what he called a ring to hold all my parts inside until the surgery. About two days later, I found out what he meant. The bladder and bowel started to fall out, again. Yep, I was having an out of body experience. The ring was not working as it was intended. It felt like you would imagine a fellow feels, with extra stuff between your legs. How do they do it? I went off to the doctor's again. He moved up the date of the surgery to the next day. The surgery was a success, but they had trouble waking me up. I was so comfortable. It was the very best sleep I can ever remember having. They persisted, and I woke up finally.

When I opened my eyes, I saw fish. Blue, red, yellow and green. Then there was a multicolor clock and a huge stuffed mouse on the table next to my bed. My daughter Tori was sitting in the chair waiting for me to wake up. She smiled and said that the OB/GYN ward was full, so they put me in the pediatric ward. I wasn't crazy, after all.

Just before last Christmas, I was rushing across the parking lot at church, to a choir rehearsal. I tripped on a crack in the sidewalk and went flying. I landed very hard on my left side. Somehow I had flipped in the air, because I was going right. I hit the concrete so hard both of my shoes fell off. It took me a few minutes to compose myself before I continued inside the church. My complete left side was throbbing, from my hip to my ankle. I found my shoes, and slowly put them back on. My left wrist was hurting by that time, but there was no blood anywhere. Hobbling into the church, the pain started to subside. When I got into the choir loft, of course, my friends asked why I was late. I told them that I had just fallen in the parking lot. I was limping ever so slightly and they thought I was joking. I am such a card. By the time we left the rehearsal, the pain was gone from my side. All the next day was spent trying to figure out exactly what had happened. I had fallen so hard that I had no memory of hitting the cement. Why didn't I break something? Finally, I heard myself mutter "thanks". The pain has not returned to this day.

Chapter twenty:..Now That Reminds Me..

It's Friday night and that brings to mind the second car I had. Actually, it was the second car that Dave and I owned. My mom had given us a car for a wedding present. The blue and gray 1946 Pontiac. It was in excellent condition, and it was like taking a little bit of home with me to South Carolina. Dave thought it was an old fogies car, and wanted to trade it for a 1950 Ford he had seen at a local car lot. It had dual glass packs, and could go from zero to sixty in three seconds. Since it seamed so important to him, I said "OK". I was surprised to find myself really happy with the car. I was the one driving it most of the time, since I had to take Dave to the base and then go to my part time job at the local movie theater. I got really proficient with the speed shifting that Dave insisted the car was adjusted for. It had belonged to a local stock car driver and he customized it for his leisure driving. The glass packs had a low growling rumble when the car idled. The guys couldn't believe that a young blond, girl with pony tail flying in the breeze, knew how to control such a rad car. I would stop at a red light and guys would pull up next to me and smile and say, "Hey, wanna drag"? At first I just laughed and ignored them. But, I found myself saying "sure", and then I would leave them in the dust. It was all quite exciting until one evening Dave had caught a ride home with the guy next door. He heard the car come down the street and a screech as I pulled into the drive and drove around the house and came to a stop, as if on a dime. He was waiting for me in the doorway. I had some explaining to do. The results of the long talk were that I promised to change my ways, and start acting like a responsible adult. It was funny to see him (the boy who cut off the parking meters in the town square as a prank) lecture me (the girl that was the secretary of the youth temperance council, junior chapter; the Red Cross volunteer; and president of my church's youth group) just the year before.

Well, I was behaving like a juvenile delinquent, so we agreed to trade the car for a more suitable one. We bought a 1952 Buick roadmaster. It looked like a blue tank and weighed about two thousand pounds. I certainly could do no wrong in that beast. I hoped and prayed that I would never get stuck anywhere, cause I certainly could not push it.

Dave felt sorry for me and decided I had learned my lesson, and so we traded again. This time he found a little Oldsmobile coupe that looked like a family car, and wasn't too sporty. I decided I wanted to go home to be with my family to await the birth of our first girl. Dave was on a mission in Africa at the time, and I didn't want to be alone so far from home. So, I went home to Ohio and we sold the car to Dave's cousin. The next car we got was a 1947 Studebaker. It was a green car that looked the same front and back. It was hard to tell if it was coming or going, if you looked at it quickly. Although it was a fine car (I wasn't a mechanic by any stretch of the imagination), and I forgot to check the oil for a couple of months. It went dry and burned up the engine. The next car was our first, while not our last, Volkswagen. It was an OK car, but the brakes failed. We couldn't afford to get them replaced. We learned how to stop by coasting and by pulling the emergency brake. We got quite good at improvising. As at that time, our family was growing, we discussed the situation and decided the only rational thing to do, was trade.

Next came a Chevy that we didn't even get paid before we got orders to Germany. We couldn't take the car out of the state, because our loan was with a local car dealership. So, we returned the car to them, and left town.

I visited my mom and family while Dave found us a place to live and got a new car (I use the term loosely) in Germany. When we met Dave in Germany, he took us from the airport out to the car. Despite the long and tiring trip, I almost got back on the next plane to the states right then and there. The car was so nondescript I couldn't believe it. It was box shape, steel gray (with no frills). It was left over from WWII. By no frills, I mean, it was the outside, the motor, and two rows of seats. After all, he had paid the GI that was returning to the states, a whopping fifty dollars. It ran on isopropyl alcohol, and you had to double flood it, to get it started. When Dave re-enlisted a couple of months later, we bought a new Volkswagen station wagon. It was so cool, and safari beige.

Wow, our first new car. What a status symbol that was. When we brought it back to the states, we were the envy of all, because VW's were very scarce in the US. Which meant that parts were hard to get, if you broke anything, anything at all.

Not long after we returned to the states. Dave was transferred again, and the children and I were not to be left behind. We sold the VW and bought a Mercury Marquise, a pink (also known as the Pink Panther) tank this time. Then there was a Ford, another Buick (and a horse also), then three VW's (one square back and two bugs), a Chevy Impala (an elegant ladylike car, that I loved), a Rambler stationwagon (whose interior was designed by Gucci and was appropriately named the Green Hornet), and a huge Chevy station wagon (the third row seat faced the back of the car). The grandchildren loved that feature. So, when all the children were grown, Dave and I decided we could have our own motorcycles. That is what we did. (Dave, Tori and me) I customized our helmets. Dave had owned motorcycles before, but this a first for Tori and me to attempt. I found it very exhilarating. I especially liked it when I would arrive at my destination, pull off my helmet and shake my head. I had a full head of long blond hair, and I got a lot of strange looks. People were not as understanding or tolerant of young women riding motorcycles as they are now-a-days.

When we went to live in Colorado, I was not too keen on riding in the mountains, and Dave agreed. We sold the motorcycles, and drove

David's (my son) Buick. He'd joined the Air Force, and was transferred to Germany. He didn't need a car there because he lived on base.

The next car we bought was a dark blue Chevy Impala. And when the truck fell on top of it, we got a brand new Volkswagen bus. It was the champagne edition, with quartz clock and all the frills this time. It had a fold out bed, a table, fridge, stove, curtains, closet, with water and electric hook-ups for camping. It was strange driving though, because the steering wheel was right in the windshield.

Since Dave's gone I have had a couple of cars of my own. The first one was a little Pontiac firebird. A sporty white car with red interior. On a mountain trip, the engine threw a rod and that was the end of that car.

Next was a Mercury Grand Marquise, beige and beautiful, with everything automatic.

When the engine gave out, I got a little gad about Toyota Corolla. It was very light and maneuverable in traffic, plus it was gold. A very chic car.

Then I traded it for a Camry. When it gave out, I decided that I did not want a car anymore. I drive Gaye's car these days. Officially, at this time, I am without wheels. It is OK though, I am trying to decide what there is out there that I haven't tried… So many cars…..So little

time………

When we were first married, all Dave could afford to give me was half a dozen roses. So he continued through our marriage to give me half a dozen roses. And I loved it.

Chapter twenty one.Now That Reminds Me.

Most people tend to look for a lifelong partner that they are compatible with. Hence why the new internet match makers are so popular. You tell about yourself in your video and what you would like in a partner. Some videos include what you do not like in a partner.

We used to call those "pet peeves".

In high school we had "slam books". They were not allowed in school, which is part of the reason they were so popular, I think. We used a steno pad so they would look like an ordinary part of our homework notes. A person's name would be written at the top of the page, and then the pad would be passed around for comments. You could write complements or blasts about the person on the page. It was perfectly anonymous, of course. It was always scary to find your own name on the pad. Sometimes, depending on the comment, we would disguise our handwriting. Just in case a book got detained by a teacher. On the inside cover of the pad was the secret code to tell who the owner of the pad was.

These days, kids have so many different avenues of technology to choose from to gossip about the other kids. It's truly amazing to me.

If you are of the belief that high school is the training ground for the rest of your life, then marriage (if it fits into your life plan) is an integral part of the rest of your life. It was for me, but I was not ready for marriage. I had too many things to do, to see, to be; to get involved with anyone that could weigh me down.

Dave and I were as different as night and day. Maybe that was what made him so exciting to be with. We could talk about any subject; he was into mythology and I was into art and travel. He liked to cut off parking meters downtown, and remodel his friend's cars; I liked playing tennis and drawing. But we could appreciate each others likes and dislikes. When we touched, there was a chemistry that could not be denied.

When he went off to basic training we missed each other very much. The letters flowed, every day, both ways. He made the big decision to stay in the Air Force for twenty years while he was there. He wrote that he wanted us to do the tour together. I had to think about it.

All the while I could not stop thinking about the fantastic possibility of seeing the world. Traveling with someone that I cared a great deal about. My personal plans would have to be put on hold (and would in all reality never be fulfilled). So, of course, I threw caution to the wind and said "yes". Wouldn't you have?

Marriage......

The first year was spent trying to please each other. But, that is so exhausting!!!!!!!!!!!

The Air Force actually saved out marriage, I truly believe that with all my heart. The constant separations made it difficult to have long range fights. We had to make up so he could deploy. We were never sure how long he would be gone and we had to leave each other with happy memories. He called as often as he could. Being the airborne radio operator, he could call me anytime the plane was in the air. His calls were very comforting to me. I would pass on messages from the other guys to their wives. It made the time apart seem shorter to the both of us. The next few years were spent concentrating on our little ones.

Dave and I now had another set of differences to address, discipline. We had such a hugely different approach to discipline. That was when we came up with the idea to have two different households. When he was home, we used his rules and when he was gone, we used mine. Thank goodness our children understood the situation from a young age, and adapted so well. They were so great, that sometimes I think they raised the two of us.

As the years went by, I wondered if marriage would change us and we would grow more alike in our perspective. Not a chance! Dave had a gambling problem (bad), and would engage in day-week long poker games. While he was very good, he lost too much. He was our sole support, and quite often he lost everything we had. It was especially bad when he would re-enlist and loose his bonus before the kids and I would even see it.

After one of his big games, he came home and handed me a wad of money. It was a thousand dollars. In the sixties, that was more money than I had ever seen, at one time, in my life. I took it and hid it. I made us a reservation in Amsterdam, got all the info on the exciting things to see there. I had a list of twenty seven things to do and see in Amsterdam by the time we left the house. It was a great vacation for me and the kids (Dave said he had a good time too). There was one draw back to the trip, Tori's allergies went into a rage, and her eyes swelled shut on the third day. We had to leave early, but it was still a great vacation.

When Dave went on one of his game fits, I would get so mad, I'd slam every door in the house about a dozen times and then go for a long walk. I would come back and try to figure out what we could do to get back to normal, one more time. Sometimes, if he didn't come home in a day or two, I'd corner one of his buddies and interrogate him until he'd confess where the game was. I would show up and embarrass him so much, he'd leave before he lost too much. Sometimes I'd wonder if he had a secret wish to loose, because he was a good player. But when he lost, it was always big, and something that we couldn't afford for him to do.

My vice was traveling. If there was a bus leaving the base, I was on it. When we lived in the village of Beerstadt, whenever the landlady's husband (he was a firefighter, and worked one day on, two days off) and Dave were working at the same time, we'd pack up the kids (she had a little girl the same age as Tori) and go out sightseeing in the countryside. At night, we'd put the kids to bed, knit and drink a little wine. She spoke about as much English as I spoke German, and we would tell each other stories and knit, drink and laugh all night long. When our husbands were at home at the same time, we would cook out in the courtyard. We would play charades, pass the wine and talk (there was a lot of sign language), laugh until the neighbors would hang out their windows yelling at us to "halt, bitte". It was a very delightful time for all of us. We still exchange Christmas cards with them.

Marriage, now as in the past, is more than a beautiful ceremony and a honeymoon. It is something that two people work at and maintain the special feeling (the itch that can not be satisfied by anyone else but your husband) for a lifetime. It is relating to others as a pair, a set, and a combo if you will. It is becoming as a unit without either person giving up their own identity or dreams. You incorporate those elements into the marriage.

As I told you in chapter one, Dave had a massive heart attack. The coroner told me that he was dead before he hit the floor. I could have not revived him. It happened two months before our wedding anniversary. On the morning of what would have been our anniversary, there was a knock at my front door. When I opened the door, the man standing there had a package in his hand. He asked if I was Dave's wife. When I nodded yes, he gave me the package. He was a friend of Dave's, a jeweler at the base exchange. I opened the package, it was a diamond ring. I felt suddenly faint. The poor fellow looked at me wide eyed as I sunk slowly toward the floor. He caught me and helped me to a nearby chair. After a moment I had started to regain my composure. Then he told me that about six months before, Dave had told him I'd never had an engagement ring of my own. I had his mother's ring. One day when I was washing clothes (at that time, by hand), and hanging them out on the line to dry, I had lost the main stone out of the ring.

It had rained the night before, and the ground was mud. We searched and searched but, could not find it. I was devastated. Dave and his whole family would hate me forever. Dave calmed me down by promising that he would have, at some point, the stone replaced for me. But over the years, it was forgotten. He decided, that this was the year, I should have my own ring. He arranged for the ring to be delivered to me, at the house, on our anniversary. So, that is what he was doing. The jeweler had thought he should have brought the ring to me when he heard about Dave's death. He reconsidered and followed the original plan. I was so happy that he did.

Our 25th anniversary. Dave had the gold tree in the background made for me.

This little rock we stood on was Dave's idea of mountain climbing. Then the kids and I would climb the rock behind us in the picture

Chapter twenty-two.Now That Reminds Me.

I am fascinated buy the way things change from generation to generation. Check out these modern conveniences Every time I refill the dish washer, I am reminded of the way we used to wash the dishes by hand. At family gatherings, mostly holidays. We would form a line across mom's long kitchen, and pass the dishes from table to sink and then from sink to cabinets. It was a great opportunity to socialize and get the dishes done fast.

Raising babies has changed radically, too. Some examples of that are: when my children were little you put butter on a burn, not now; baby's first foods were bananas and orange juice, and once again, not now. As we were growing up, every year we attended about four fairs; a couple of county fairs, and the state fair. Now a days, it's theme parks. While the same basic idea is present, things are so elaborate now. The roller coasters are bigger and wilder. I much prefer to sit by and watch all the bags and the strollers. I wave as they whiz by, and pretend that they can see me from an up-side-down position. In reality I'm the blur just past the orange ball. And the price is the most elaborate thing of all.

The technology now a days is out of sight, it has changed so fast.

When I was a teenager my family was one of the first on our block

to get a TV. It had a nine inch screen and only had programs after

six pm. We had to keep the light off in the living room while the

TV was on, so we could see the screen. Some of my friends, who's

parents had not bought a TV yet, would just casually drop in to

visit and watch a little TV. Another plus was that the programs

were live.

It was an exciting time alright. And the exciting times keep

coming. I have finally given in to computers. Until about ten

years ago, I had to have someone turn the computer on for me. I

took some classes and now, I can turn it on myself, and I even have

an email account. Now that's convenient.

Convenience, now that reminds me......... During the military

service period of our lives, we lived in a few places where the

mountains were conveniently close to us. We could climb, hike

and camp at will (well, when Dave was home, that is). The base

had an equipment rental store. They had all the equipment you and

your family need for a weekend outing in the nearby hills. Dave

was in the Air Force, and was a great airborne crew member, but

he was not an avid outdoorsman. We once had our picture taken

as he and I stood on a rock (about two feet above the ground) and

said, "OK, I have climbed a rock for you." The kids and I would
climb the mountain, and Dave would have his lawn chair, cold
beer in his ice chest and a good book to read. He would wait for
us at trails end. We would romp on the mountain trails for the day,
and tell him all about it when we descended to base camp (as we
laughingly called it). We repeated this process in South Dakota,
California, the Ozarks, North Carolina, and Germany.

Of course things were different when we were near the Ocean, lake
or river. He was a great swimmer, water skier, and fisherman. In
those instances the tables were turned. I was the one that sunk like
a rock. So, I would lay in the lawn chair and read while I tanned.
We were the opposite in the tanning department too. He looked
outside on a sunny day and turned the most beautiful tan. On the
other hand, I used the tan without the sun lotion by the bottle, and
if I was lucky, I'd have a tan by August. The whole process was
extremely amusing to watch.

And fortunately, we kept our sense of humor close at hand. When
it came to our tempers, we were opposite too. He was a yeller, and
had an excellent way of turning the innocent defensive. He could
also deliver a lecture at the drop of a hat. Pick a subject and he had
a lecture for it. The kids quite often fell asleep during his lectures.
Now that's a long lecture.

My anger management called for door slamming. Gnashing of

teeth accompanying the demonstration, to be sure. When I had my fill of slamming, I would exit the building and walk it off. When I returned, the particular subject was never mentioned again, in my presence that is. I'm sure the children laughed about the fit for days. Dave got his opinion out in the open, while I kept it pent-up inside. It festered, until my body rebelled and I had a nervous breakdown. The military doctors would give me a shot, some pills and send me home. I'd quiet down, and be just fine for a while. Then the process would start all over again. Mostly it turned out that it was time to transfer to the next base. We would get a new start at the next base. We were too busy getting moved and settled to address the old issues. As the years passed, we both mellowed slowly. After about twenty-six years, we were more tolerant of each others faults. We started concentrating on the good qualities. That was a positive step in the right direction. And I truly believe that is all we can hope to achieve. I have never attained the perfect life, or the perfect me, but I have gotten a little wiser. Thank you for coming with me on my stroll down memory lane. It was my pleasure to share my highs and lows with you. I started as a naïve teenager and evolved into an understanding mature woman. I am still learning.

Out behind our house in Colorado. I could go there to think and relax.

Misc.......

As a last note, I would like to share with you a short list of medical terms and definitions that we re-defined as an interoffice chuckle. We were working on the medical journals, and needed a break. See if any of these terms ring a bell with you.

Artery…..the study of paintings

Bacteria…the back door of a cafeteria

Barium….what doctors do when the patient dies

Bowel…...a letter like A, E, I, O and U

Caesarean Section….a neighborhood in Rome

Cauterize…made eye contact with her

Coma…….a punctuation mark

D&C…….where Washington is

Dilate……to live longer

Enema……not a friend

Fibula…….a small lie

Tablet……a small table

G.I.Series…a soldier ball game

Hangnail….a coat hook

Impotent….distinguished, well known

Secretion….hiding something

Medical Staff..doctor's cane

Nitrates……cheaper than day rates

Node……..was aware of

Outpatient…a person who has fainted

Pap Smear..a fatherhood test

Tumor……..more than one

Recovery Room…a place to do upholstery

Rectum…….dang near killed 'em

Printed in the United States
128489LV00002B/54/P